D1326860

The
STORIES
of SCIENCE

Integrating Reading,
Writing, Speaking,
and Listening into
Science Instruction,
6–12

JANET MACNEIL
MARK GOLDNER
MELISSA LONDON

Foreword by Karen Worth

HEINEMANN
Portsmouth, NH

Heinemann
361 Hanover Street
Portsmouth, NH 03801–3912
www.heinemann.com

Offices and agents throughout the world

Library of Congress Cataloging-in-Publication Data
Names: MacNeil, Janet, author. | Goldner, Mark, author. | London, Melissa, author.
Title: The stories of science : integrating reading, writing, speaking, and listening into science instruction, 6–12 / Janet MacNeil, Mark Goldner, and Melissa London.
Description: Portsmouth, NH : Heinemann, [2017] | Includes bibliographical references.
Identifiers: LCCN 2017022509 | ISBN 9780325086774
Subjects: LCSH: Science—Study and teaching (Middle school).
Classification: LCC Q181 .M19 2017 | DDC 507.1/2—dc23

LC record available at https://lccn.loc.gov/2017022509

Editor: Katherine Bryant
Production: Vicki Kasabian
Cover and interior designs: Suzanne Heiser
Cover photograph: istock / Getty Images Plus / man_kukuku
Typesetter: Shawn Girsberger
Manufacturing: Steve Bernier

Printed in the United States of America on acid-free paper
21 20 19 18 17   PAH   1 2 3 4 5

CONTENTS

FOREWORD

One has only to read the introduction to this book to know that this will be a book driven by the authors' enthusiasm about science and their joy in science teaching and learning. This wonderful book combines theory and practice to present an exciting addition to the literature about inquiry-based science teaching and learning—the use of story. In their words, "A good science story is like a riveting adventure story or mystery. It's so enthralling that the audience members are immediately drawn in because they feel like they're right there beside us, discovering something new and exciting. They can understand what's going on and see how it connects to their lives" (page 14).

Several things struck me as I read this book. The authors are adamant that a critical purpose of science education is to stop the cycle of negative views of science in our society today. This means that students must develop knowledge and understanding and, at least as importantly, they must learn to love science, to understand how we know what we know, and to be able to communicate what they know in engaging ways to different audiences. Janet, Mark, and Melissa assert that this can be accomplished through inquiry-based science with the idea of story at its core. This is not the story of fiction. It is a way for scientists, young or old, to "make a strong connection to the audience by sharing their curiosity, enthusiasm, and personal ideas—essentially sharing a part of themselves along with the science" (pages 2–3).

The authors engage us with the importance, the joy, and the nature of science stories using their own and students' stories as examples.

When students create stories, they do not just improve their literacy skills; approaching science this way can lead to enriched and effective inquiry-based science teaching and learning.

This is a book by and for teachers, and the authors provide advice, guidelines, scaffolds, and examples for using story in your classroom. Story becomes a catalyst for highly effective and authentic inquiry-based science. The authors pay their respects to the best teachers, research in science teaching and learning, literacy instructional strategies, and more. This is not an abandonment of the best of inquiry-based science teaching and learning; rather it offers a new lens that increases the power of inquiry-based teaching.

Just as we think we're done, the authors take us to one more delightful and exciting place. They "zoom out and highlight a fourth type of story that is just for teachers: the instructional stories of science" (page 139). Now we see how a unit, a year of study, and multiple-grade sequences all can be crafted through the lens of story.

I can't help thinking about how artfully the authors themselves have created a story about using stories. The book itself has the basic elements of story: it has an intriguing question or problem, a theme or big idea, key evidence, a strong conclusion, and a specific audience. That audience is science teachers, whom I encourage to read this engaging and important book to find out what stories they and their students can create.

Karen Worth

ACKNOWLEDGMENTS

Like every good science story, this book began with a question: How can we learn how to weave science and literacy together to deepen understanding (as well as engage students) and share what we learn with our colleagues? We'd been trying out many different approaches in our classrooms and really needed some guidance. How lucky at this point that we crossed paths with our soon-to-become mentors: Karen Worth, Jeff Winokur, and Martha Winokur! Their guidance and modeling helped us develop a deep understanding of how the tools of literacy can be used to support science. We began to apply this newfound knowledge in our classrooms and saw for ourselves the positive changes that it brought about for our students and ourselves. No longer did literacy feel like an added burden—it became an opportunity! We created a graduate-level science and literacy course for our district (with the incredible support of the Brookline Education Foundation, to whom we owe an enormous debt of appreciation), began giving presentations at conferences, and ultimately got the opportunity to share our ideas in this book. Many thanks to Karen, Jeff, and Martha for getting us started on this journey.

We also want to acknowledge our incredible Brookline colleagues for your willingness to dive into new things, try them out, and selflessly share your work and ideas with each other. We're so proud to work and learn with you! In addition, we want to thank our past, present, and future students—you inspire us, teach us in many ways, and are at the heart of everything we do (you might say that you are the main characters in our stories).

Writing this book was also a deep learning experience for us. Our editor, Katherine Bryant, did a fabulous job of helping us capture our ideas and experiences and guiding us toward thinking about them in new ways. As we attempted to practice what we were preaching (applying the elements of good science stories and targeting our purpose, audience, and setting), you kept us on track and gave us valuable, insightful feedback. We greatly appreciate your help and expertise, and we have become better storytellers as a result of working with you.

JANET

Most of all, I would like to thank my husband, Ian (my fellow science soul mate and life explorer), who constantly sparks my curiosity, inspires me, helps me grapple with my never-ending supply of questions, talks me calmly through the rough spots, and always helps me see the light at the end of the tunnel. My story would not be complete without you.

MARK

It is through this book that I honor my late father, Ronald Goldner, who instilled in me a love of science and teaching. He was always interested in the stories behind the science, and throughout the process of putting together this book, I imagined many wonderful conversations with my father. Most of all, I hope that in some small way, in the spirit of my father, this book inspires others to be creative and to do good things through the teaching of science.

MELISSA

An English language arts teacher at heart, I was sweaty-palmed when my principal asked me to switch gears and begin teaching science many years ago. This book represents the essence of what I have always felt to be true: it is not literacy or science; it is literacy and science. Thanks always to my students; you inspire me to want to find the stories that make teaching and learning a delight.

INTRODUCTION

Stories have power. They delight, enchant, touch, teach, recall, inspire, motivate, challenge. They help us understand. They imprint a picture on our minds. Want to make a point or raise an issue? Tell a story.

—Janet Litherland

We love science and sharing our passion with students. But we've also come to realize that you can't do science without applying strong literacy skills (reading, talking, writing, and listening). As we grappled with how to do this in our classrooms, the light bulb went off! What would happen if we used the concept of story to weave literacy skills into what we already teach in science? Wouldn't this be a great way to bring these two disciplines together in a meaningful way instead of just jumping through the literacy hoops without any context?

So, instead of fighting the push to weave literacy into science, we have embraced it—searching for ways to use it to make science more engaging, deepen understanding, and help our students become more effective science communicators. Our journeys started in different places (as you can see from our personal stories that follow) and have converged around our willingness to improve our practice and to try out new things. Just like in science, our path of discovery is never finished. (That's what makes it fun!)

Our Fundamental Question

Every science story starts with a question. In this book, we're seeking to answer this question: How can we teach students to communicate about science effectively? There's a lot to unpack within this overarching question:

- What are the stories of science and why should students tell them? (Chapter 1)
- What are the features of effective science stories? (Chapter 2)
- How can we help students find questions that they want to tell stories about? (Chapter 3)

- How can we use model stories to show students what exemplary science stories look, sound, and feel like? (Chapter 4)

- Why is it important for students to consider the purpose, the audience, and the setting behind each story? (Chapter 5)

- Why do scientists craft explanatory stories and how can we help students do this on their own? (Chapter 6)

- How can students create informational science stories to teach and excite others about what they've learned? (Chapter 7)

- What are the personal stories of scientists? How can we draw students into the content via these stories, teach them to craft the personal stories of science, and engage them in creating their own science memoirs? (Chapter 8)

- How can we thread instructional science stories into our curriculum to create a coherent and meaningful structure for learning? (Chapter 9)

In this book, we share our stories, strategies, and experiences with integrating science and literacy—practices that are having a strong positive impact on our students and our teaching. Our goal is to foster a generation of students who understand science (how it is done as well as the people who do it) and can effectively communicate about it. We hope to inspire you to try out some of these strategies on your own. As Sylvia Earle said in the film *Chasing Ice* (2013), "It isn't just the drive to climb mountains and hang off cliffs [that makes a difference]. . . . It's the ability to capture it and communicate it. Observing and knowing is one thing. Sharing it and sharing it effectively can change the world."

Our Personal Stories

To start off our adventure into science stories, we'd like to share what kindles our passion about science, teaching, and telling the stories of science.

Janet's Story: The Curious Scientist

It was my dog Luna that found it. Always on the lookout for something "good" to roll in, she had uncovered a skeleton buried in the side of the cliff by the ocean. What was it? How did it get there? So many questions bubbled up in my mind as we carefully dug it out. Of course, I had to take it back home and investigate it further—drawing it and recording all my questions and ideas in my science notebook, measuring it, and cleaning it up (it still had quite a pungent odor!). Based on my observations, I figured out that Bruce (as my daughter named it) was an adult harbor porpoise. It's this kind of thing that has earned me a reputation as the crazy science lady—something that I'm really proud of. I feel so lucky that my natural curiosity and wonder about the world is as great today as it was when I was a small child.

My path has taken many turns. Inspired by my love of nature (fostered by my father and oldest sister), I studied earth science and environmental engineering and worked for many years as an engineer, environmental consultant, and science technical writer. It wasn't until I started volunteering at my children's school (creating math and science nights with my husband and doing outdoor classroom work) that I realized what I was meant to do: teach science. I dusted off my curiosity, my desire to know how things work, and my love of learning to embark on a new adventure. Over many years, I have been able to draw upon all my past experiences (as well as new ones) to focus on ways to improve teaching and learning as well as share my infectious passion with students and teachers so that they can view the world through the wonders of science too. This includes creating curriculum that actively involves students in learning how to ask questions and investigate to find the answers on their own, builds a deep understanding of big ideas (instead of focusing on discrete facts), provides a glimpse of who scientists are and how they work, and teaches students how to effectively communicate science in ways that are interesting to their audiences.

Mark's Story: The Intrepid Explorer

It's December 2007, and I'm standing on the back deck of the *Nathaniel B. Palmer* icebreaker, several hundred miles off the coast of Antarctica. The boat is rocking violently in the twenty-plus-foot-high swells. Barely visible beyond the floodlights of the ship, I can see the inky blackness of the water interrupted by white foam. The energy and chaos of the deep polar ocean is unmistakable. I struggle to keep my balance, but in my hands is an essential piece of hardware and rope that I will pass on to the rest of the team as they begin to hoist oceanography equipment over the side of the ship. Suddenly a huge wave crashes over the deck, swamping us all. I slam against the guardrail and barely manage to hold onto the scientist next to me.

Fortunately, we all end up unscathed (but wet and cold) from this rogue wave. Later, we are able to laugh about the experience (and learn from it!). But as I regain my senses, I wonder, *How did I end up in this place (considering that I started out as such a shy little kid)?*

I grew up in the comfortable middle-class enclave of Lexington, Massachusetts. Every summer my family and I would spend several weeks at our summer cottage on the coast of Maine. I spent my time exploring by myself along the amazing tidal bay in front of our little house. While I did my share of collecting and exploring the various shells, sea glass, and other detritus, what always fascinated me was the sheer power and speed at which the tide came and went every day. My favorite moment was when the low tide suddenly turned, and water would begin rushing into the bay. I would dig complicated dams and tunnels and observe how the water would slowly eat away at these earthworks and inevitably overwhelm them. It is no wonder that I decided to pursue physics in college!

What draws my interest in science is its stories. Sure, it's useful to know the names of different plants and rocks, but I've always been more interested in the stories behind these objects. Why was it that the same two rock types (brittle schist and hard, crystalline granite) were visible up and down the mid-Maine coast? Why did these rocks change as we travelled inland, up toward Baxter State Park? The slow but dramatic story of geologic transformation along the New England coast has inspired me to learn more about the rocks in our area. How did scientists figure out that such dramatic changes occurred? What was their evidence? Could I see it myself?

The cottage and its peaceful and beautiful setting was a wonderful place to get away and recenter ourselves; this was most true for my father, who chose our property and designed the house. An engineer and scientist, my dad was always searching for answers to nagging questions about the world. Early in his academic career, he had wanted to be an astronomer, but he pursued engineering instead; he wanted to use his scientific talents for practical ends and to help improve the world. "Make the world a better place than you found it," was his oft-used mantra.

My father's stories were often aspirational. "Imagine if we could live in a fossil-fuel-free world . . . ," he would often muse and then launch into an excited description of the world as it could be—one that he was actively trying to bring about through his research into passive solar and battery technologies.

These stories have drawn me deeply into the world of science and have led me to participate in several research projects as a teacher-scientist. One of these landed me on the oceanography research vessel in December 2007, as we delivered a set of instruments to the ocean floor in an attempt to tell the story of how a warming atmosphere might be affecting the ocean currents surrounding the Antarctic continent. Understanding the story of climate change has become a central passion of mine. Through PolarTREC, I've gone to Svalbard, Norway, and Denali, Alaska, to work with and learn from scientists to try to unravel the details of our changing world.

It is through my own authentic experiences with science that I've become passionate about the stories of science, and I hope to help teach the power of science stories to my students.

Melissa's Story: The Master Storyteller

Let's just say I came to science later in life. My elementary science education was spotty at best, and in fact, before being asked to teach fourth-grade science and then later sixth-grade science, I hadn't done any science or really thought about science as a discipline since sophomore year in high school, when I failed my midyear chemistry exam and was allowed to drop the course. I even managed to avoid taking a single science class during my four years at Smith College. I'm not proud of this, mind you, but it is the truth. So how did I come to be a dedicated sixth-grade science teacher at my K–8 school in Brookline, Massachusetts, cowriting a book for middle and high school science teachers, you ask? A fair question. The answer is simple: An English language arts teacher at heart, I discovered that I loved science once I started to think about science through the lens of story. Leveraging the power of story has helped transform my approach to learning and teaching science.

The stories of science are timeless. They are populated by would-be heroes and villains and full of mystery and intrigue, adventure, danger and discovery, failure and triumph. For my students who have grown up in the age of sequels and even prequels, science never needs to get old; there is always more to understand. Chapters in science are constantly being revised and rewritten. Approaching science as story has made all the difference in my own experience of coming to science later in life, as both a student of the discipline and a teacher. Charged with inviting middle schoolers to step outside of themselves for a spell and explore ideas central to science, I decided to contextualize their learning in terms of story, to inspire them to ask and answer their own questions as they develop their own stories of science to share.

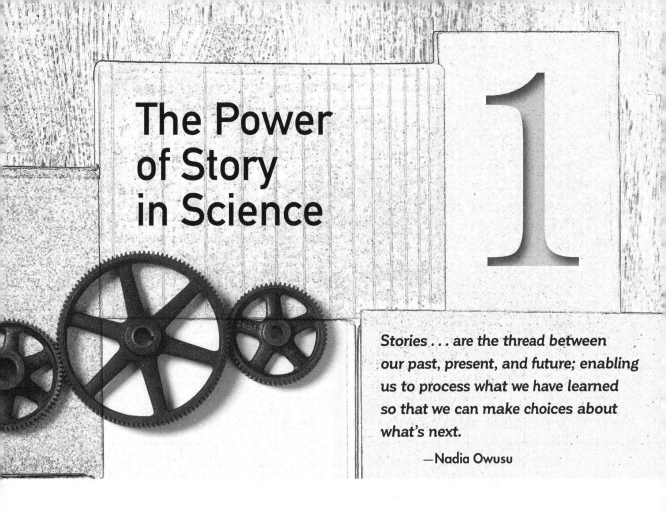

The Power of Story in Science

1

> *Stories . . . are the thread between our past, present, and future; enabling us to process what we have learned so that we can make choices about what's next.*
>
> **—Nadia Owusu**

A Story from Janet

As a child, I was a voracious reader. (I also was lucky because I had three older sisters who loved to read aloud to their little sister.) I inhaled mysteries, comic books, poems, picture books, and our Book of Knowledge set (an encyclopedic series of beautiful leather-bound volumes chock-full of stories, science, history, and poetry). My father was also a natural storyteller. I remember listening to him talk about growing up on a small farm in the hills of Pennsylvania, living off the land in order to survive. The images that he painted of my grandmother churning butter and milking the cows and of my father and his brothers hunting and tracking game (including bears) in the woods are still vivid in my mind, even though I never visited the family farm. I realize now that my love of learning and curiosity was shaped by these early experiences with story—they were a key part of how I learned about the world.

Just like the memorable stories that Janet grew up with, science stories are often filled with interesting characters, captivating plots, conflicts, and a sense of mystery or discovery. But underneath, they are still grounded in authentic, real-life science. Science stories are not fiction but are designed to communicate about science in ways that will fascinate the audience and make our curiosity and passion contagious. We can harness the powerful elements of story to help students learn about science by sharing the exciting stories of science and enticing them to take center stage by telling their own science stories. In this way, students can become personally and actively involved in creating the larger story of science as they use key literacy skills (writing, reading, talking, and listening).

In future chapters, we dive deeply into science stories: the elements of good stories, how to use model stories to showcase those elements, how to spark questions that lead to stories, how we can build the use of each type of story into our classrooms, strategies for teaching students how to tell their own stories effectively, and how to weave instructional stories into teaching. But, as with any good story, we need to start at the very beginning: What are science stories and why should we use them when teaching science?

Why Bring Stories into the Science Classroom?

Throughout human history, we have told stories to educate, entertain, and inspire others. The art of telling the stories of science is not that different. However, some people may balk at the idea of telling stories in science—after all, stories are fictional, right? Not really. As Anne E. Greene says in *Writing Science in Plain English*:

> Many scientists see little connection between communicating their science and telling stories. They think of stories as made-up, while science is based on fact. However, to most writers, "story" simply describes a powerful way to communicate information to an audience. Recent research has shown that our brains are wired to recognize stories with a particular structure, one that features characters and their actions, and information presented this way becomes compelling and memorable. Scientists can use these same elements of stories—characters and actions—to write about the real world with the same desirable results. Writing stories about science doesn't mean making it up or dumbing it down. Rather, we can hang complex ideas on the scaffolding of good, simple stories and make our science as exciting to our audience as it is to us. (2013, 12)

Scientists tell stories for many reasons: to explain phenomena, teach and share information, and learn from the tales of other scientists and their discoveries. Stories may also be designed to persuade or build excitement about science. In the process of telling stories, scientists make a strong connection to the audience by sharing their curiosity, enthusiasm, and personal ideas—essentially sharing a part of themselves along with the science. Imagine what will happen when we strategically weave these authentic science stories into science teaching and learning!

Just mention the word *story* to your students. Right away you'll have their attention. In addition to grabbing students' interest and curiosity, telling the stories of science in class and teaching students to compose their own stories will give them the big-picture context of the content they are learning and empower them to be effective communicators. Most importantly, you'll be modeling and teaching the authentic use of stories in science and making the stories relevant to them and their lives.

Story is also an effective way that people organize and store information. In fact, we remember information that is embedded in a story much more effectively than information that is shared in lists or lectures without the context of a story. Researchers have found that when science content is embedded in a story that allows middle school students to "vicariously experience the scientific journey of discovery," students have a deeper understanding of the content and retain the scientific concepts longer (Arya and Maul 2012, 1030). In this study, researchers asked one group of students to read scientific information in a narrative (story) form that included the aspect of scientific discovery and asked another group to read the same information presented in a more traditional textbook fashion. The researchers measured student comprehension and recall for the information in the text immediately after students read it and again one week later. The data suggest that student understanding and recall was significantly better for the group that read the story versions. These findings indicate that weaving the element of story into our teaching will increase not only student engagement but their understanding as well. In addition, stories build personal connections to the content, scientists, other students, and the audience. As a result, when students incorporate story into all the ways that they communicate about their work as scientists, their connection to their audiences will be much more compelling.

The Messiness of Science Stories Fuels the Creative Process

Science stories don't always have neat-and-tidy endings. When reading fictional stories, people often like and expect a happy ending where all the loose ends come together in a satisfying conclusion. Sometimes that happens in science, but most often we are left with even more questions, discouraging results, and some level of frustration. When we do this work with students and ask them to tell a story explaining their findings, for example, students sometimes try to force fit their results and explanations so it all comes out neatly. We need to encourage them to be true to the evidence and be objective, no matter the outcome.

We also must help students recognize that often many different stories can be told from the same set of data. This leads to lively discussions about the strength of evidence and the resulting explanations. Students may even change their thinking and refine their stories based on the ideas of others. It is this type of rich discourse that has led to new scientific discoveries and acceptance of scientific theories over time.

In short, science stories can be messy, but that's what drives us to learn more, think about the questions in different ways, and persevere to create stories that can be complex and provocative.

Science Stories Strengthen Students' Literacy Skills

Science teachers today are being asked to support students' literacy development in ways we haven't been before. The Common Core State Standards for English Language Arts (NGA Center for Best Practices and CCSSO 2010), and similar standards adopted in other states, explicitly require teachers to integrate reading, writing, speaking, and listening into the content areas. Students are expected to integrate ideas from multiple sources and justify claims based on what they read; write explanations, informational pieces, and narratives of many kinds; and effectively communicate their ideas orally in discussions and presentations. The stories of science provide an authentic opportunity for you to seamlessly weave these critical skills into your existing science instruction and curriculum.

What Are the Stories of Science?

The world of science has many different types of stories to tell. Science stories can be used to

- make meaning (explanations of phenomena, or explanatory stories),
- teach others or share information (informational stories), and
- share the stories of scientists and discoveries (personal stories of discovery, changes in science over time, individual scientists, and how science is important in our lives).

The types of stories often overlap and can be combined in many different ways. For instance, students may construct explanations based on hands-on investigations, do research using other sources to extend their learning, and then add additional information (informational stories) to their explanatory stories. This mimics what happens in the real world when scientists write papers based on their research. In addition to their results, they typically include overviews of research and findings by other scientists as background. The context helps them see how their data fit into the larger puzzle (or perhaps rock the boat!). To make the experience even more personal, students can research the scientists behind the major discoveries revealed in the informational stories, as well as scientists who are currently seeking answers to new questions. What drives them? What are their struggles and how do they overcome them? How did they find out and prove ideas that we now widely accept as truths?

When the three types of story are combined, the full story emerges: our explanations of a phenomenon (based on our own firsthand inquiry), additional information that we gathered from other sources to supplement our research, and the background of the scientists that did or are doing this work themselves. For culminating projects, especially at the high school level, it would be incredibly powerful to have students paint this complete mural of a topic—putting all the individual panels together. Figure 1.1 summarizes the three types of science stories.

Types of Science Stories			
Story Type	**Purpose**	**Why This Type of Story Is Important in the Science Classroom**	**Examples**
Explanations: Claims based on evidence connected by reasoning	To explain a phenomenon based on firsthand observations, investigations to answer a question, or both	Students make meaning of data using higher-order thinking skills, deepen their understanding of science concepts, and clarify the story of a phenomenon to answer a question in their own words.	Analyze and interpret data on the properties of substances before and after they interact. Make claims based on this evidence to answer the questions, Did a chemical reaction occur? Why or why not?
Informational stories: Summaries of research that has already been done on a topic prior to an investigation, short articles for a broad audience, briefs on a new scientific discovery, field guides, visuals (e.g., posters, infographics)	To synthesize information from other sources (other than firsthand observations or investigations) to inform others (informational research)	Students synthesize information from other sources to answer questions that they cannot answer via firsthand investigations, identify key information, and clearly communicate what they learn in a way that is understandable to their audience.	Describe how the periodic table can be used to predict and design combination reactions that result in ionic and molecular components. Focus question: How can the periodic table be used in real life?

continues

Story Type	Purpose	Why This Type of Story Is Important in the Science Classroom	Examples
Personal stories: Narratives	To share stories about scientists (including student scientists) and their discoveries as well as how and why the ideas of scientists change over time	Students learn how scientific discoveries are made, how scientists work, and how science changes over time. They also have the opportunity to reflect on their discoveries and growth in science.	Compose an engaging story of how and why Dmitri Mendeleev developed the periodic table. Focus question: How and why was the periodic table developed?

Figure 1.1 Types of Science Stories

Explanations: Stories That Answer Our Questions About How the World Works

Science focuses on seeking answers to questions we have about the natural world. What causes tides? Why do compasses point to the north? We observe and investigate in order to find answers to these questions and then use our data to explain what we have observed. Scientists discuss different (and often opposing) explanations to collaboratively identify what the strongest answer to the question might be. This process of argumentation (discussed in Chapter 6) strengthens our stories as we share and critique them, deepening our understanding of the topic.

The various stories that scientists create to explain the world are fascinating and they change over time as new evidence is gathered (often made possible through the invention of new tools). In the classroom, students can construct explanations in two ways. They can craft science stories that explain the world based on hands-on inquiry (see Figure 1.2). These inquiries involve conducting experiments or making observations (e.g., examining a fossil and making inferences about the organism and its environment). We believe that this type of hands-on inquiry should be the main focus of science teaching and learning at all ages. When students are constructing explanations based on their own data, they are actively participating in the authentic process of science. Alternatively, if firsthand inquiry is not possible (because of physical or material constraints) students can analyze data collected by other scientists and construct explanations from that.

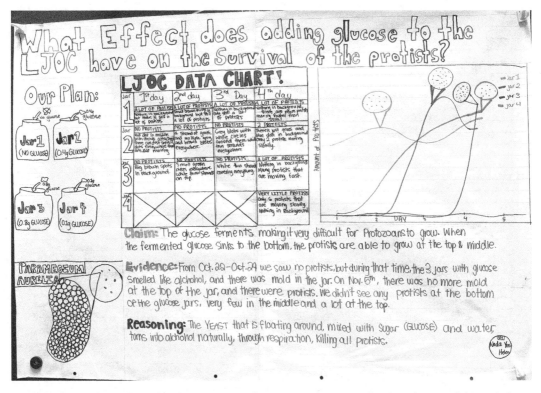

Figure 1.2 Seventh-grade students grew protists from grass clippings in water. They used these "little jars of crud" (LJOC) to design and investigate their own questions. Students shared their explanatory stories based on their investigations with the class via visually appealing posters.

See Chapter 6 for more details (and specific lessons) on intertwining stories that explain the world into your teaching.

Informational Stories: Stories That Teach Others

In addition to sharing results based on inquiry and hands-on investigations, scientists often share information that they have synthesized from other sources (other than from firsthand investigations). Teachers may also ask students to create informational stories to assess understanding.

We use effective informational stories in the classroom all the time to introduce concepts and extend the learning of our students beyond the school walls. For instance, television programs like *Bill Nye the Science Guy*, *Nova*, and *Cosmos* bring science to life for students. Among other things, these types of media can be used as model stories to show how scientists can effectively share information. (We discuss model stories in more detail in Chapter 4.) For more specifics on informational stories and lessons for teaching them, go to Chapter 7.

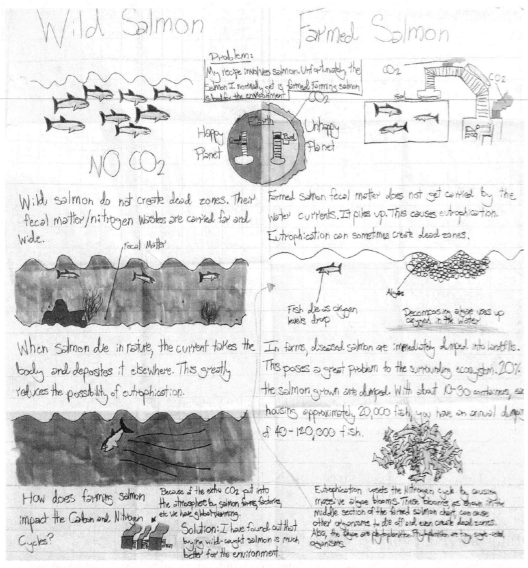

Figure 1.3 Infographics such as this student example about wild and farmed salmon are one type of informational story.

Personal Science Stories: Stories of Discovery

Everyone loves a good adventure story. When you think of it, the stories of science and scientists often are filled with adventure, discovery, conflict, and perseverance. How can we bring these stories into the classroom to engage our students and provide them with the rich backstories behind the concepts they are learning? How can we engage them in sharing their *own* stories of exploration and discovery?

The personal stories of science can be told from many different perspectives in various ways. Students can craft them to describe

- why science is important to them in their daily lives,

- the features of scientists and how they do their work,

- the discoveries (and failures) of scientists and how they overcome roadblocks, and

- how students themselves practice the skills of scientists, the features of scientists that they exhibit, and how they can use what they learn to explore answers to their own questions (in and out of school).

Personal science stories like the following example written by a student, using information from an article by the editors of Biography.com (2016), make the interesting discoveries and passions of scientists come to life.

Jacques Cousteau

Thanks to Jacques Cousteau, the world got the chance to see the beauty and wonder of the ocean with our own eyes before many of us had had a chance to experience it firsthand. Jacques Cousteau was a marine biologist. He was born on June 11, 1910 in France.

When he was a boy his arms weren't as strong as a normal child so his doctors encouraged him to swim in order to build up his strength. He turned to the ocean and found out that he adored the sea.

Jacques Cousteau loved to tinker and to build all sorts of things. His inventions were so elegantly designed, that millions could follow him into the deep. He made the first underwater camera and with that he made the first full-length, full-color underwater film. This was the first time some people had ever seen what was inside the ocean before. Cousteau brought live coral, moray eels, and whales into people's living rooms. . . .

Jacques Cousteau became a very important voice for protecting the oceans. During his explorations of the oceans, Cousteau found that the seas had been changing as a result of pollution; marine plants and animals were dying at an alarming rate. He started the Cousteau Society which is still active today. Its mission is to educate people about the importance of the oceans and the need to protect our seas from pollution.

In addition to telling the personal stories of other scientists, it's also critical for students to reflect on themselves as scientists, what they have learned about science, and how they learned it. Following are some questions that might guide their reflections:

- *The importance and changing nature of science*: How is science relevant to my life? What are the tools of science and how do they change our ideas about the world? How has my thinking about science changed?

- *Science practices*: What are the skills of science that I use? In what ways have my skills improved? What do I still need to work on? What characteristics of a scientist do I have?
- *Science content learning*: How did I learn science content? What did I do and what kind of thinking was involved? What evidence of my learning can I provide?

Self-reflections, like the one that follows, help students realize that they are working and thinking like scientists, and they show students that they are active participants in their own learning. In addition, having the chance to think reflectively lets students become aware of their strengths, areas for improvement, what helped them learn best (hands-on activities, science talks, online discussions, etc.), and what they might need to do differently next time. When we consistently incorporate self-reflections into science teaching, students build their self-confidence and awareness that learning how to *do* science (instead of memorizing content) is the key to lifelong learning.

> Simply "knowing things" is sufficient, but I believe having an inquizitive [*sic*] mindset and being capable of asking and answering your own questions is crucial when studying science; whether it be physics, biology or astronomy. Over the past two years I have undoubtedly developed as a scientist, student and crtitical thinker through countless experiments, projects and unsatisfactory grades.
>
> As a child, I was always fascinated by the world. My parents would take me to the planetarium and I'd fall asleep that night wondering what life was like in a parallel universe. I would spend my summers outside searching for bugs under rocks and trying to figure out why they could fly and I was constantly being held down by some force called gravity that I was not yet able to comprehend.
>
> What I craved was an outlet where I could harness my thoughts in a more formal setting as opposed to keeping all of these discoveries and questions I had generated bottled up in my head. It was around fifth or sixth grade when science became an organized subject and I had finally found my outlet.

Strategies for involving students in learning and sharing the personal stories of science are provided in Chapter 8.

How Can We Integrate All Types of Science Stories to Deepen Learning?

Although the different types of science stories have different purposes, they are ideally used together in the science classroom to create an even stronger overarching story of a concept or phenomenon. This strategy works with almost all science concepts; here we provide a specific example focused on the life cycle of stars.

When studying the life cycle of stars, we begin by having students perform a hands-on inquiry of electromagnetic spectral data around the focus question, How can we use the spectra of a star to determine its characteristics (such as composition, age, and size)? Students observe the spectra of sample stars and make claims based on the evidence collected to determine what elements (e.g., hydrogen, helium, and heavier elements such as oxygen or nitrogen) were present in the stars' atmospheres. They also infer the stars' likely color, temperature, and age based on the spectral information. They construct explanations to make sense of their data (claims based on evidence connected by reasoning), share these stories via face-to-face or online science discussions, critique them, and learn from each other to revise and strengthen their own explanatory stories.

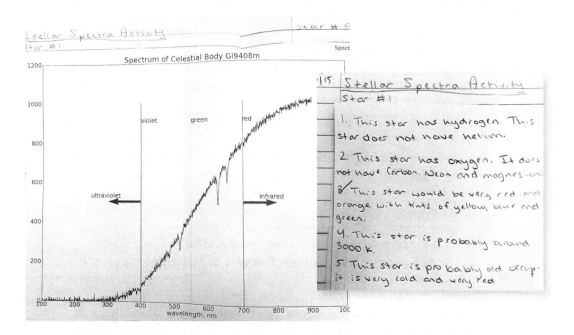

Figure 1.4a–b A student's initial work toward creating an explanation based on stellar spectra

This process generates intriguing questions about the life cycle of stars and how we know what we do about them, including the tools scientists have used in the past and are developing for the future. Students use other resources (e.g., reliable websites, books, videos, and interviews with experts) to gather additional information. They synthesize their findings in different ways, such as in posters, videos, podcasts, and illustrated text. A variety of online communication tools can be used too. For example, a Prezi presentation about how stars die and the tools scientists have used to study this part of a star's life cycle can be accessed via https://prezi.com/scenkqza5xy_/stars/?utm_campaign=share&utm_medium=copy.

After creating their explanatory and informational stories, students craft personal stories about scientists who studied stars (or are studying them now). They pick scientists of interest to them, then research what questions their scientists were studying, what they did to seek answers to their questions, what they discovered, as well as their struggles and how they overcame them. The following excerpt is from a student's personal story about Celia Payne.

Celia Payne Discovers What Stars Are Made Of

Celia Payne was born in Wendover, England, in 1900. Her father died when she was only four. As a result, Celia was exposed to a strong woman figure at a very young age as her mother raised three children on her own. This exposure allowed her to understand that a woman can do anything that a man can do, and it guided her ascent to one of the most accomplished scientists of all time.

When she was 19, she was granted a scholarship to Newnham College of Cambridge University where she discovered her love and interest in astronomy. But, the college did not grant degrees to women at that time, so she was not granted a diploma. In 1923 she ventured from England to Harvard, which gave diplomas to women.

At Harvard, Payne's intelligence was recognized by Harlow Shapley, and he persuaded her to write a doctorate. Her doctorate was finished in 1925 and was titled, "Stellar Atmospheres, A Contribution to the Observational Study of High Temperature in the Reversing Layers of Stars." In doing her research, she discovered that the sun is actually made of much more different elements than the earth. This hypothesis was contrary to the beliefs of that time. She discovered that hydrogen was the most common element in the universe, something that we know to be true today but was considered radical during her time. Due to the fact that her ideas were new and unconventional, astronomer Henry Norris Russell tried to persuade her that her thesis was wrong.

Ironically, four years later, Russell found the same theory was correct. Even after Payne's work was accepted, Russell is often given the credit for the discovery. Nevertheless, her thesis is known as one of the most brilliant astronomy theses ever written.

By blending the explanatory, informational, and personal stories of science into the content, we give students the chance to grapple with the idea of how we know what we know about stars themselves (just like scientists do), research answers to questions that come up along the way, and then get a glimpse of the people who built or are building our current understanding of stars. This rich array of information provides a strong foundation for their future questions and learning.

The Essential Elements of Good Science Stories

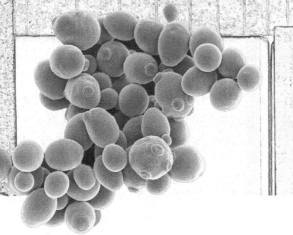

Good science stories are no different than good stories about anything else—they're just a great read.

—**Helen Pearson**, chief features editor for *Nature*

A Story from Mark

While working with a class on an Internet-based research project about elements and the periodic table, two of my students were frustrated with what they were reading. "Doing research in science is so much harder than doing research in social studies!" one student said, and the other agreed. This exchange led to a very interesting conversation with the class.

"All the websites are boring," said one student.

"I'm having a hard time finding the important information," said another.

We determined that most of the information on the web about this topic was simply presented as lists of facts, without a good story to tie the facts together. The students contrasted that with a recent research project in their social studies class. "There's usually a good story we can follow," a student said. We brainstormed what made a good story, and students agreed that a good story has a well-defined narrative, complete with characters, a buildup of suspense, and some element of surprise. This lack of good story elements, indeed, seems to be what is missing from many of the readings about science.

A good science story is like a riveting adventure story or mystery. It's so enthralling that the audience is immediately drawn in because they feel like they're right there beside us, discovering something new and exciting. They can understand what's going on and see how it connects to their lives. In essence, all the elements of a good story (of any type) are there; the difference is simply that the focus is on science.

As we mentioned in Chapter 1, science stories are not dumbed down or fictional; they are authentic explanations, informational media, and stories of science and scientists based on real research data and facts. The difference is in the way these stories are told. They are related in a way that makes them more interesting and accessible to wide audiences.

Some people may balk at the idea of applying the elements of good stories to science. Why do we think that's so important? Traditionally, scientists have focused on communicating information clearly and in a format that is accepted by scientific journals or at conferences (i.e., by their scientific colleagues). This mode of communication has been translated into middle and high school classrooms, where a major goal has been to teach students to share their findings in the classic lab-report format. This is a very useful skill and one that we value.

However, we feel that there is an urgent need to shift this approach so that the focus is on communicating about science to a broader audience. Instead of just targeting other scientists in a format that only they may understand, why not share the same information in a way that is down-to-earth, visually appealing, and understandable to the general public? This is an invaluable skill for students to have if we are going to break down potentially negative public misconceptions about science and scientists. If people are able to understand and get excited about science, they may not be skeptical or afraid of it. Our students need to be able to craft science stories in a way that invites other nonscientists into our fascinating world and widely spreads scientific ideas to a global audience. Actor Alan Alda (visiting professor, Alan Alda Center for Communicating Science at Stony Brook University in New York) says:

> Whenever I would be at a university where they taught science, I would try to talk the president of the university into the idea of teaching communication while they taught science, because if you can graduate experienced scientists, capable scientists who are also capable communicators, then the public has a chance to learn something from them. . . .
>
> I think when we see scientists as human beings, the door is open for us a little bit, we can go into their lives. They're not the white-coated gurus on the mountaintop. (Grant and Lamberts 2016)

Ingredients for a Good Science Story

A man dressed in Arctic-weather gear is climbing down into a bottomless abyss in the Greenland ice sheet to photograph an enormous waterfall cascading down into the earth. This is James Balog, an environmental photographer who has installed cameras on glaciers and ice sheets in Iceland, Greenland, Alaska, and Montana to collect visual evidence of changes in glaciers over time. He hopes that these powerful time-lapse images of glaciers "dying" will convince the public that climate change is not a hoax. As he says, "the story is in the ice somehow."

The project, documented in the movie *Chasing Ice* (2013), presented several engineering challenges because the delicate camera equipment needed to be protected from the brutal environmental conditions of the Arctic (hurricane-force winds, falling rock, and subzero temperatures) and mounted on the sides of mountains. At first, the cameras did not work—they were buried in snow, the batteries exploded, and there was a fatal flaw in the timers. After extensive troubleshooting, Balog replaced all the timers and the cameras began working successfully, capturing evidence of striking recession of glaciers over several years.

Can you pinpoint what makes this an engaging and interesting science story? These are the four critical elements:

1. *An intriguing question or problem*: What is happening to the world's glaciers and ice sheets over time? What challenges do scientists face when gathering data in harsh environments and how do they overcome them?

2. *An overarching theme or big idea*: Ice-covered areas of our planet are changing drastically.

3. *Key evidence*: Photographs show that glaciers and ice sheets are melting over time.

4. *A strong conclusion*: Time-lapse images that Balog collected over several years at multiple locations substantiate the claim that glaciers and ice sheets around the world are melting at a rapid pace. (*Note*: Some science stories may not have neat-and-tidy endings like this one did. Perhaps the data are inconclusive or conflicting. In those cases, the conclusion should summarize the issues with the data and recommend next steps or further questions to be investigated.)

Not all science stories may be as action-packed and exciting as *Chasing Ice*, but they should include these elements. (Additional elements may be important for different types of stories, as we discuss in further detail later.) Let's think a little more about what these key elements look like, using the model story "Turtle Shells May Not Have Started Out as Body Armor After All" (based on a 2016 article by Lyson et al.).

Turtle Shells May Not Have Started Out as Body Armor After All

We all know that the purpose of turtle shells is to protect them, right? This may be true for modern turtles, but a new interpretation of fossil evidence may show that turtle shells didn't initially evolve for protection after all. Instead, the precursor to the turtle shell (thick ribs) may have helped the animals dig burrows, according to Dr. Tyler Lyson, a paleontologist at the Denver Museum of Nature and Science.

To understand Dr. Lyson's research, we first have to know a little bit about turtle shells. They're not like the shells of other animals (which typically create their shells by adding bony scales on top of their bodies). Instead, turtle shells are actually *part* of their skeletons! As turtles evolved, scientists believe their ribs, sternum and spine fused to form the shell. Over time, the ribs got broader and broader, until they finally fused together as found in more recent turtle fossils. (To see an animation of how Dr. Tyler Lyson believes this process occurred, based on fossil evidence, go to: https://www.youtube.com/watch?v=NphNApmSZ0U.)

While Dr. Lyson was studying turtle fossils, he began to question the widespread belief that turtle shells developed for protection. It just didn't make sense to him. He noticed (as you can see in his animation) that the ribs of turtles began to get wider and wider over time before they eventually fused together to form the shell. But, the broader ribs didn't really provide much protection to the turtle until they were fused (like they are in modern turtles). In fact, the wider ribs made it harder for the turtle to breathe (since ribs and connected muscles help inflate and deflate the lungs) and move (because larger ribs limited the flexibility of the trunk, shortening their stride and making them move slower). So, Dr. Lyson wondered: Was protection the reason why shells began to develop in the first place?

To explore this question, Dr. Lyson and his team studied many fossils of the earliest known turtle ancestors, the *Eunotosaurus africanus* (found in South Africa about 260 million years ago). The scientists observed that the fossil reptiles had a short, triangular skull, big claws, bone structures that indicate powerful forelimbs and triceps, as well as thicker ribs—features similar to present-day animals that dig and burrow (like the giant anteater and burrowing gopher tortoise). Strong triceps would have given the animals the ability to dig with substantial force. Dr. Lyson believes that the broader ribs provided stability to the animals (anchoring the front legs) in order to allow them to dig with their strong forelimbs. Cross sections of the legs also show that the front legs (the "shovels") were made up of very thick bone, but the back legs were not. Finally, based on the size of fossil bones around the eye (sclerotic rings), the scientists believe that the animal had small eyes, which may have been able to see in low light situations, such as those underground.

Fossils from other ancient turtle species have been found to have wider ribs and big claws as well. But other scientists think that more evidence is necessary to support this explanation.

Dr. Lyson's explanation has sparked even more questions, such as why did the turtles burrow? He thinks that this behavior may have allowed them to survive in the very dry and hot conditions that existed in South Africa at the time. Going one step further, Dr. Lyson wonders if the ability to burrow may have kept the early turtles from extinction during the end-Permian mass extinction (about 250 million years ago).

This research provides some intriguing new ideas about why turtle shells evolved—fostering a lively debate among scientists. It is an excellent example of how scientists use fossil data to attempt to explain why adaptations change over time in response to environmental conditions. As more fossils are discovered, additional evidence will help determine which way the turtle shell argument goes.

Intriguing Question or Problem

Scientists are driven by the intriguing, deep questions that motivate us to find out more and attempt to explain what we observe. Consequently, these questions or problems should be the focus of the stories we tell.

A good science story starts with a meaty question for students to ponder and investigate. At first, we can provide these questions. But our ultimate goal is to entice students to come up with these questions on their own—questions that they will want to investigate and then share with others in the form of stories.

What kinds of questions provide the seeds for growing good science stories? The best questions cannot be answered with a simple yes or no; jump-start critical thinking (not just a regurgitation of information or facts); and are intriguing. For instance, the question in the turtle shell story is, Why did turtles develop shells? (a question that was inspired by the discovery of new fossil turtle evidence).

More examples of intriguing questions (and not-so-intriguing questions, for comparison purposes) are provided in Figure 2.1. We dig deeper into this topic in Chapter 3.

Comparing Questions for Science Stories

Intriguing Questions	Not-So-Intriguing Questions
How do the unique features of water allow life to survive on Earth?	What are the physical characteristics of water?
What forces cause Earth's surface to change over time? What effect do these changes have on humans?	Does water affect Earth's surface?
If all living things are made of cells, why don't they all look alike?	What are the parts of cells?

continues

Intriguing Questions	Not-So-Intriguing Questions
How are the living and nonliving parts of the Earth system connected? What happens if one part of the system changes?	What is an ecosystem?
What is the relationship between matter and energy?	What are the states of matter?

Figure 2.1 Good questions for science stories are meaty and intriguing.

Overarching Theme or Big Idea

Every good story needs a theme (which we call a big idea). This big idea is closely connected to the question and identifies what the story is about. In the turtle shell example, we explore the question (Why did turtles develop shells?) with a provocative explanation based on the fossil evidence. The big idea is that turtles may originally have begun to evolve with thicker ribs (the precursors of modern-day turtles' shells) in order to dig burrows so they could survive in hot and dry environments.

After identifying the big idea, we need to make sure that it is the focus throughout the story. Including extraneous information that does not support the big idea leads to long, convoluted stories that are not effective (and become boring).

Key Evidence

Science isn't magic! We can't just say something is true without backing it up with strong, relevant evidence. Our stories must include that evidence, whether it's derived from firsthand investigations or gathered from other sources.

The evidence in the model story includes fossil evidence of thicker ribs, bone structures that indicate strong triceps and forelimbs, sharp claws, and small eyes that may have been able to see in low-light situations (such as those underground). These features are similar to the characteristics of some existing animals that burrow.

Strong Conclusion

A strong finish is critical for any type of story. We don't want to leave the audience hanging. Instead we need to reiterate the big idea, why we believe it, and perhaps its relevance. In many cases, a story may end with further questions to explore.

At the end of the model story, we acknowledge the scientific debate that this new explanation will fuel (especially as new fossil evidence comes to light) and refer to the relevance of using fossil data to attempt to explain why adaptations change over time in response to environmental conditions.

Other Story Elements That May Come into Play

In addition to the four essential elements (question or problem, overarching theme or big idea, evidence, and conclusion) that apply to all science stories, students may need to consider additional elements, depending on the type of story they're creating (see Figure 2.2).

The audience will also determine the need for certain elements. For instance, some people may argue that explanations don't need snappy titles, engaging hooks, and vivid language. However, we think they do—*if* the purpose is to share information with certain audiences (such as the general public, younger children, and so on). On the other hand, if the intended audience is a group of scientists, or the teacher's purpose is to have students learn how to write classic scientific lab reports, some of these elements might not apply. In Chapter 5, we talk more about tailoring stories to the target audience.

Element	Description	Type of Science Story
Key Elements of All Science Stories		
Intriguing question or problem	The compelling question or problem that the story is about	Explanatory story Informational story Personal story
Overarching theme or big idea	The idea that is the focus of the story (related to the question or problem)	
Key evidence	Evidence that explains the story and shows the audience why the story is relevant	
Strong conclusion	Clear summary of the big idea or message as supported by the evidence to leave the audience with a lasting statement	

continues

Element	Description	Type of Science Story
Other Elements (May Vary Depending on the Type of Story)		
Snappy title	Title that grabs the interest of the audience and tells what the story is about	Explanatory story Informational story Personal story
Attention-grabbing hook	An opening that immediately captures the audience's attention	Explanatory story Informational story Personal story
Compelling, clear visuals	Photos, tables, or graphs that illustrate the essence of the story, clarify details, or even can tell the story by themselves	Explanatory story Informational story Personal story
Appealing characters	Characters (both human and nonhuman) that make the story come alive	Informational story Personal story
Interesting setting	Details on where the story takes place	Informational story Personal story
Exciting sequence of events (plot) with tension	A story that plays out in logical order with some conflict or tension to build interest	Informational story Personal story
Voice and grammar	A voice and a tone that target the audience, are clear, and use juicy adjectives and adverbs to paint vivid pictures in the minds of the audience; correct grammar	Explanatory story Informational story Personal story
Structure	Logical flow that is concise and clear	Explanatory story Informational story Personal story

Figure 2.2 Key elements of science stories may differ, depending on the type of story.

The use of these elements in science stories is described in more detail in the following chapters.

Tips for Keeping the Audience on the Edge of Their Seats

Many of the elements of good science stories are meant to grab and hold the attention of the audience. (After all, what value is a story with no audience?) In the movie *The NeverEnding Story*, a boy reads a magical book and finds himself falling into the fantasy world described by the author. This is exactly what we want the audience to do when they read, hear, or see our science stories.

Take a look at the following story about fire ants, based on articles by Yong (2011) and Bai (2011). What is it about the story that captures and keeps your interest? Why?

Fire Ants Engineer Their Own Escape Rafts

What happens to most animals during floods? They run away or get swept away by the floodwaters, right? Not fire ants. These ingenious insect engineers build their own living rafts to save themselves from drowning.

Individual ants are denser than water (and would normally sink). But when fire ants form a raft, they hang onto each other using their sharp mandibles, claws and adhesive pads on the end of their legs. This traps air bubbles—giving the unlucky ants on the bottom of the raft air to breathe and decreasing the density of the raft substantially (by up to 75 percent). As a result, the raft floats like a dream—often for months if needed. Ants also naturally repel water because they have a waxy coating. This makes their raft waterproof too!

Why do you think the fire ants have adapted this behavior? Well, it turns out that they nest in soil in moist areas. These habitats are often flooded, leaving the ant nests underwater. Their ability to sail away from harm is the only way they can survive.

Several strategies are used to lure readers into this story (and keep them there):

- Start with an interesting hook (a question in this case).
- Include clear, concise details that are key to the big idea, question, or theme and make it interesting.
- Explain the science simply and clearly (and provide context when necessary).

- Convey a sense of curiosity and excitement or wonder throughout.
- Choose colorful adjectives and descriptors to create vivid mental pictures for the audience.

We talk more about using model science stories (model stories) to teach students how to use the elements of good stories in their own work in Chapter 4.

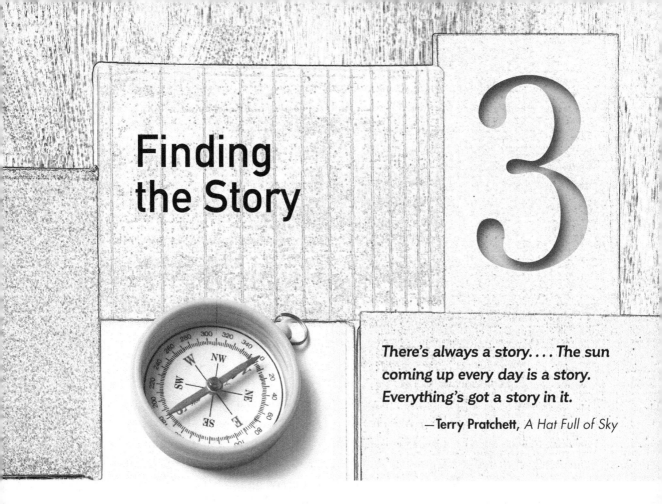

Finding the Story

3

> There's always a story. . . . The sun coming up every day is a story. Everything's got a story in it.
>
> —**Terry Pratchett**, *A Hat Full of Sky*

A Story from Mark

"How can we possibly know all that stuff about the universe?" a student asked me a couple of years ago. (This was after a lesson on the size and scale of the universe, at which point students realized just how vast the cosmos is and how little of it we've been able to explore.)

The question led to a profound shift in my own thinking about astronomy. I realized that what makes astronomy a fascinating story is not the details of what we know, but how we know it.

Now the question we explore in class is, How do we know what we know about the universe? This question inspires students' imagination. They ask deep questions, like, "How far can telescopes see?" "Is a manned mission to Mars realistic?" and "Could we ever get close enough to a black hole to study it?"

I had unwittingly stumbled upon a fantastic narrative. The universe is incomprehensibly large, and we are stuck on a tiny rock in one small corner of it. Even so, we have been able to unlock some of the secrets of the universe.

Science and its stories are driven by questions (and not just any old question will do!). Fine-tuning the right questions to spark student interest and teaching students to master the art of questioning is at the heart of effectively using stories in our classrooms.

Curiosity and Imagination

Questions drive science and science inquiry instruction. We are really good at providing questions and the means to answer those questions; that's the essence of most activities in the science classroom. But how can we extend these activities and use them as jumping-off points to push student thinking and spark even more questions that then become the seeds that germinate into students' stories of science?

We believe that shifting teaching toward student questions and stories doesn't require a radical shift in teaching practice. You don't have to abandon your tried-and-true activities! Instead, you can open up the wealth of ideas that you already have in your teaching tool kit to reveal the stories that lie underneath. Student questions are the key to doing this. You can start by allowing time for students to ask questions (honoring and inspiring their curiosity), share and discuss their ideas around these questions, and then investigate and research the questions throughout the unit of study. If we give students the right materials and resources to engage with their questions (ones that lead them to the questions we want them to be thinking about), they will most likely come up with questions that tie in directly to our instruction. (Other questions can be documented and saved for future use, as we talk about later). Then, these student-generated questions can become the focus of hands-on investigations, research for informational stories, personal reflections, and stories about the scientists who worked or work on these topics.

Types of Questions

The types of questions that students generate will determine the kind of stories that might emerge:

- *Explanatory stories:* Questions that can typically be explored by doing hands-on investigations may lead to explanatory stories. These questions have variables and cause and effect embedded in them. In some cases, students may use data that have already been collected by others to answer an investigable question and craft an explanation.

(They may also gather information from other sources following their investigations to create informational stories.)

- *Informational stories:* Questions about things and phenomena that we cannot observe ourselves lead to informational stories. We need to call upon the research and resources collected by others to answer these questions, which may include questions about space, undersea creatures, or plate tectonics.

- *Personal stories:* Questions about other scientists may lead to personal stories of science. These include stories about their work (their results, how their thinking has changed over time), what sparked their questions, how they worked, what they were like, and so on.

Ways to Inspire Student Questions

There are many ways to help students come up with questions that will lead to good science stories. We have found five approaches to be particularly effective and adaptable to a wide range of classes, ages, and topics:

1. Unpacking big questions
2. Transforming traditional activities into inquiries
3. Helping students find questions that they can investigate to create explanatory stories
4. Facilitating student-to-student talk
5. Using formative assessments to uncover student thinking and questions

Unpacking Big Questions

Questions that we can easily answer are never as interesting as those that make us ponder. To inspire student questions and inquiry, we want to avoid questions that can be answered with yes, no, or a regurgitation of facts. Instead, we need to teach students to craft really big, essential questions and then unpack them to uncover all the other questions that lie within.

Examples of essential questions that are worth unpacking are listed in the text box on page 26. What makes them ideal for inspiring further student questions? First of all, these questions are really big: there are lots of concepts and ideas that we need to know about in order to answer them. They also are intriguing, so much so that students really want to think deeply about them and will have many questions about what kind of information might be needed to answer them. Finally, these questions are complex and novel—questions that will make students think about the topics in a new way because they probably have not encountered questions like these before.

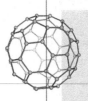

Examples of Essential _Questions_ That You Can Unpack with Students

- Why are there so many different kinds of plants and animals on Earth?

- Why are the shapes and sizes of leaves so different?

- If all living things are made of cells, why don't they all look alike?

- How has life managed to survive on Earth for the last four billion years (through meteorite impacts, climate change, and continental movement)?

- How do the unique features of water allow life to survive on Earth?

- How do we know how old Earth is and what happened during its past?

- What forces cause Earth's surface to change over time? What effect do these changes have on humans?

- How does energy from the sun drive processes that occur on Earth?

- What is the relationship between matter and energy?

- In what ways are all ecosystems the same?

- How are the living and nonliving parts of the Earth system connected? What happens if one part of the system changes?

- How do living things survive in a changing environment?

Putting It into Action in Melissa's Classroom: A Deep Dive into Unpacking Questions

I recently asked my sixth-grade science students to consider the following question: "What can studying the ocean floor tell us about whether or not there is life on other planets?"

Hands shot up. Before taking any of their answers, I asked them, "What do you think are some other questions that we might need to ask and answer in order to address the first question in an intelligent and sophisticated manner?"

Some hands that were up went down, and several new hands rose. I recorded the new sub-questions students raised:

- What is it like on the ocean floor?

- What lives on the ocean floor?

- What else do you need for life besides water and air?

- What are other planets like?
- How are the ocean floor and outer space the same?
- How can we find out information about places we haven't been able to get to yet?

Then I asked students to turn and talk to one another about their ideas related to these questions. The conversations were animated—more so, I suspect, than if I had just asked them to turn and talk about the initial question about the ocean floor and "life out there" (which I feared could dissolve into a huge sci-fi and potentially silly tangent).

By thinking about questions nested within the initial big question, students have the chance to think actively about the kinds of information that might be required to provide a more complete answer and, therefore, a more complete story.

Transforming Activities into Inquiries

Another way to encourage more student questions is to change traditional science activities so that students have the opportunity to generate questions and begin to find the stories within what they're doing. The key to turning existing activities into inquiries is to encourage students to develop questions that they might be able to investigate themselves. Some possible question stems are What if . . . ; What would happen if . . . ; and Would we get the same results if . . . . Several examples of transformed activities are provided in Figure 3.1.

Essential Questions	Traditional Science Activity	Ideas for Encouraging Student Questions
How do materials move in and out of cells? Is molecular motion predictable?	Students put drops of food coloring in water to see whether water diffuses faster in cold or hot water. Students explain why the drops in hot water diffuse faster.	In addition to having students answer questions about the speed of diffusion in hot and cold water, ask them to generate a list of what-if questions: • What if the liquid were different, like oil? • What if I added milk instead of food coloring? • Would the results be the same if I added more or fewer drops? Then give students the opportunity to explore one of these questions.

continues

Essential Questions	Traditional Science Activity	Ideas for Encouraging Student Questions
How do trees drink?	Students discover how capillary action works by putting celery stalks in water with food coloring. Over several hours, the leaves of the celery become colored because capillary action draws the water up the stalk into the leaves.	Following the investigation, have students brainstorm what-if questions: • What if we tried different vegetables? • What would happen if the temperature were hotter? • What would happen if the stalks were taller? Wider? Then give students the opportunity to try out one of their questions.
Why are certain genetic traits more common than others?	Students record several physical traits that are easily observed and controlled by a single gene (such as free or attached earlobes, widow's peak, and smile dimples). They record data for themselves and for the class and then determine which traits (dominant or recessive) are more common.	Ask students to discuss whether their results make sense. If some recessive traits are more common, how might that become possible? Have students generate ideas about how to make this a more fair survey and research recessive traits that are very common to find out why they are more common.

Figure 3.1 Examples of how you can turn traditional science activities into inquiries

Helping Students Find Questions That They Can Investigate to Create Explanatory Stories

When we want students to design and carry out hands-on experiments that lead to explanatory stories, the questions need to be carefully crafted. Students often come up with questions that are hard to test (what we call *noninvestigable questions*). They may be simple how or why questions that do not include variables or any way to explore cause and effect. In some cases, we can help them turn the questions into investigable questions that lead to explanatory stories. In general, the cause-and-effect format (What effect does *x* have on *y*?) is a clear model for a good investigable question. For example, Why does the ball roll faster on the floor than on the carpet? may become, What effect does surface have on the speed of the ball? The question, Why does mold appear on bread? could become, What factors influence the growth of mold on bread? Some additional examples are shown in Figure 3.2.

Noninvestigable Question	Investigable Question
How is energy produced from burning food items?	What effect does the type of container in which the food is burned have on the measurement of energy released?
	What effect does the size of container in which the food is burned have on the measurement of energy released?
Why does salt melt ice?	What effect does the mass ratio of salt to ice have on the melting rate of the ice?
	What effect does changing the type of salt have on the melting rate of ice?
How do electric motors work?	What effect does the number of coils (in a homemade motor) have on the rotation rate of the motor?
What causes osmosis?	What effect does the concentration of glucose have on the rate of flow through the dialysis bag?
Why is the sky blue?	What effect does the relative humidity of the air have on the color of the sky?

Figure 3.2 Examples of turning noninvestigable questions into investigable questions

Are noninvestigable questions bad? Absolutely not! In fact, they can be excellent questions for the start of an informational or personal science story (as you'll see in Chapters 7 and 8), but they simply don't lend themselves to student-designed investigations. For example, Why does mold appear on bread? is an important question, and students may decide to do some research into the conditions that promote the growth of mold, but there isn't a clear controlled experiment that they can do with that question. So they will have to rely on other information sources for the answers.

In addition, students often can combine their own hands-on investigations with information from other sources. Maybe they have further questions after they complete their experiment and want to find out what other scientists have discovered, or maybe they want to explore a facet of their topic that they cannot research on their own. We encourage this type of overlap between the different types of stories!

Turning Questions in the Classroom: What Does It Sound Like?

In this exchange, the teacher is able to guide the students toward two investigable questions by helping them consider their own preexisting ideas about friction.

Student A: Here's a question I came up with: Why does the ball roll faster?

Teacher: What's one possible reason you can think of?

Student B: Friction?

Teacher: What do you think this means? Which materials have more friction?

Student A: I think it's the roughness of the surface.

Student B: I think it may be more about the ball than the floor.

Teacher: So what might you test out?

Student A: I could test friction. What effect does roughness of the surface have on the speed of the ball?

Student B: Well, I'd like to test my idea about the ball. What effect does the squishiness of the ball have on the speed of the ball?

Finding Investigable Questions: Little Jars of Crud

A fun introductory activity that we do with our seventh graders is a grass-and-water infusion, in which we put grass in a small jar of water for a couple of days (Little Jars of Crud). When students look at the water under the microscope, they see a whole micro-ecosystem teeming with protozoa, bacteria, and mold. This inevitably leads to many questions. What are these critters? Where did they come from? What do they eat? What would happen if we changed something about this setup?

After several days of observations, we have our students brainstorm more questions. Then we help them categorize their questions into investigable and noninvestigable questions (see Figure 3.3 for examples). Each group chooses one of the investigable questions to test.

Noninvestigable Questions	Student Hypotheses About the Questions	Investigable Questions
Why are there little critters moving around in the jar?	• They are searching for food from the grass. • They are reproducing and searching for spaces to spread out.	• What effect does the amount of grass have on the movement of protozoa in the jar? • What effect does the size of the jar have on the population of protozoa? • What effect does the amount of water have on the population of protozoa?
What do the critters eat?	• They eat grass. • They eat other microorganisms. • They need oxygen.	• What effect does the amount of grass have on the population of protozoa? • What effect does the type of grass have on the population of protozoa? • What effect does sterilizing the grass by boiling it have on the population of protozoa? • What effect does exposure to air have on the population of protozoa?
Can the critters survive in different temperatures?	• They can live in only a certain temperature range.	• What effect does raising or lowering the temperature have on the population of protozoa?

Figure 3.3 Generating investigable questions about Little Jars of Crud

Facilitating Student-to-Student Talk to Generate Questions

Inquiry science entices students to think deeply about what they're observing and to ask questions. How do we help students develop and deepen those questions as the core of their science stories? One effective way to do this is by facilitating student-to-student discussions, giving them the time and space to explore their ideas and to probe each other's thinking.

Imagine a whole-class discussion where the teacher removes himself or herself from the conversation and allows the talk to happen exclusively between the students. We call this whole-class student-to-student talk *science talk* (based on the work of Karen Worth et al. [2009]). In a science talk, the teacher says very little, the students do not raise their hands, and the students have an informal, flexible academic discussion. With practice over time, students learn how to participate thoughtfully in a way that draws out questions, misunderstandings, and new ideas.

The teacher is not center stage during a science talk; the students are. Accordingly, the teacher acts as a facilitator, stepping in only when students are not following the science talk norms or to interject an additional question to guide the conversation when needed. The teacher can also model the type of questions that will improve the quality of discourse: "What is your evidence for that?" "How do you know that is true?" or "Could you explain that idea again?" Misconceptions will surface, but this is generally not the time to correct them.

In order to get students to the point where they can successfully participate in a science talk, we need to:

- Have a purpose, a plan, and a targeted focus question for each science talk. Why are we doing this science talk? What ideas do we want students to share? What is the key topic that we want them to explore?

- Actively involve students in setting norms to identify group expectations, and refer back to these norms repeatedly to check in: "Are we meeting our norms?" "What did we do well?" "What do we need to work on next time?" Feel free to refer to the norms and remind students of appropriate behavior during the talk if a student is acting inappropriately.

- Make sure students are aware that learning how to participate effectively in a discussion is an important skill. Learning to speak and listen effectively is as important as learning to write effectively.

In the next sections, we share some tips on setting up for successful science talks: how to set science talk norms and create student checklists.

Putting It into Action in Mark's Classroom: A Science Talk on Condensation and Energy Transfer

During a science talk, I have my students sit in an open circle (with no desks in between) and make sure their science notebooks are close at hand. I pose a focus question and then, as much as possible, I sit back and let the students share their explanations and defend their ideas. This type of discussion allows new questions to emerge, pushes students to explore different perspectives and ways of looking at the data, and helps them develop new ideas about the phenomena they are investigating. Collectively, they develop a deeper understanding of scientific concepts.

One topic we explore in eighth grade is energy transfer. As part of this unit, students observe condensation forming on the outside of a sealed glass container with ice inside. Following this demonstration, I review the class norms for science talks (which we created together as a class at the beginning of the year) and then ask: "Why is there water on the outside of the container?" as a lead-in to a science talk. The discussion flows freely, with participation from most students.

Andrew: I think the condensation came from the ice. Somehow the ice melting gets to the outside of the container.

Martha: I think it's condensation from the outside. When the warm molecules come in contact with the cold molecules, that creates condensation.

Steve: I think water rings form from condensation on the outside of the container.

Irene: Andrew, how do you think the water could get through the sealed container?

Andrew: I'm not sure, but I don't know where else the water could come from.

Harriet: Do you think what's happening is the energy is being transferred from the outside to the inside, making the ice melt?

Steve: I think it's melting because room temperature is at a higher temperature than the ice. Maybe it wouldn't be as much condensation if it were a colder day.

continues

Jim: How would the cold get on the outside if it didn't come from the outside?

Martha: The container itself would be cold. Anywhere you felt the container. Anywhere the warm molecules touched the container.

Van: Now that I'm thinking about it, "cold" made me think condensation. I agree with your point, but I think it's because of the cold inside the container, which makes water outside condense.

Frank: Going back to Andrew's idea, I was thinking that the water can't transfer through the sealed container, so I don't know how it can be anything other than the water somehow coming out of the air. But I also think that it might have something to do with what the container is made out of.

Greta: Does it really matter if the container is sealed up or not? The point is that the container is cold from the ice in the inside; when the molecules inside the container touch the outside air molecules, that causes the condensation. But maybe there would be more water on the outside of the container anyway if it wasn't sealed up.

Jim: What if the container was bigger; would that matter?

Frank: I don't think that would make a difference. Except it might slow down the process.

Van: I'm wondering if it has to be ice. What if there was something else inside the container—something cold, but that didn't melt like ice does?

During this science talk, many additional questions that could lead to further investigations surface:

- Does it matter if the container is sealed?

- Does the material the container is made of make a difference?

- Does what is inside the container make a difference?

- Does the temperature of the room matter?

In addition, I learn a lot about what my students are thinking about condensation and energy transfer.

CREATING NORMS FOR SCIENCE TALKS

In order for science talks to be effective, students need to be aware of the rules (norms). Instead of just giving our students norms, we like to involve them actively in developing them. We use the Y-chart, a tool adopted from the Developmental Designs social-emotional curriculum (see Figure 3.4). Together students and teacher brainstorm what a respectful and productive science talk *looks like*, *sounds like*, and *feels like* and fill out the Y-chart. The norms are fluid and changeable. Before every talk, we review the norms and open them up to any modifications that students think would be important based on our previous talks. At the end of a science talk, we review: "How did we do in meeting our norms today? What might we work on to make our talks more productive next time?"

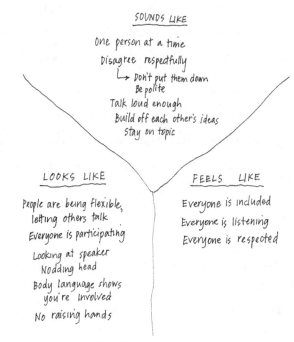

Figure 3.4 A science talk Y-chart

Sample Science Talk Checklist

Listening

- Are we making eye contact with the speaker?
- Are we acknowledging each other's opinions?

Talking

- Are we contributing our ideas to the discussion?
- Are we sharing information related to the focus question?

continues

- Are we taking risks with our thinking?
- Are we inviting others into the conversation?
- Are we making connections to what others are saying?

Learning

- Are we working together to come to a conclusion?
- Are we asking questions to help us better understand the topic?
- Are we building off of each other's ideas?

A Science Talk Planning Sheet and Science Talk Prompts are provided in Appendix A.

Using Formative Assessments to Uncover Student Thinking and Questions

Students come into our classes with all sorts of misconceptions about the world. Using formative assessments to reveal these misconceptions not only helps inform our instruction but is an effective way to engage students in a topic and to entice them to come up with good questions.

We like to use formative assessments at the very beginning of a unit. For example, prior to diving into a study of weather and climate, we might use the following formative assessment probe:

Four students were wondering exactly how the air surrounding Earth is heated up. They each had a different idea. Which student do you agree with? Explain your thinking.

Frodo: The sun's energy is absorbed by the atmosphere.

Sam: Earth's warmed surface heats up the atmosphere.

Bilbo: It's mostly energy from volcanic eruptions that heats up the atmosphere.

Pippin: Carbon dioxide in the atmosphere provides most of the heat in the atmosphere.

After giving students a few minutes to think and write by themselves, we usually have them turn and talk with a partner or small group. A whole-class science talk may be in order, especially if there is a great deal of confusion and disagreement among the students. We find that during these discussions, many intriguing questions surface, some of which may be starting points for students' own investigations or research that will lead to science stories. Figure 3.5 summarizes some possible results from a class discussion based on this assessment.

Student Ideas	Student-to-Student Follow-Up Questions
Amanda K.: I think Frodo and Pippin had the correct answer. I thought Frodo had the right answer because the sun has a lot of heat. Enough that it can warm the entire earth and it is absorbed by the atmosphere. I thought Pippin because the carbon dioxide in the air can warm Earth because there is so much of it in the world.	• I wonder how the heat gets to Earth. Does it travel all the way through space? Why doesn't the space heat up? • Why does the CO_2 heat up and not the other molecules? • Why is it hotter closer to the ground than higher up in the atmosphere?
Alec R.: The sun's light carries energy and it comes into the atmosphere and bounces off Earth and then bounces back off the atmosphere and then off Earth and so on. . . . The atmosphere acts as a one-way door, sort of. Also I think the carbon dioxide released by cars and such makes the one-way door work better (it still lets light in but less light energy out).	• I wonder why something as simple as a CO_2 molecule could let something in but not out. That doesn't make sense to me. • I wonder if the light that is going out is the same as the light that is going in.

Figure 3.5 Class discussions of formative assessment results lead to student questions.

These class discussions reveal not only student misconceptions but the thoughts and questions that spark their imagination. We can collect those questions and use them to help frame student-created science stories within the lesson or unit and our instruction.

How to Record and Honor All Questions

Students ask so many great questions, and there is a perpetual tension about whether to explore them all. If we investigate all of our students' questions, we'll never get through the content! What strategies can we use to keep track of their questions and recognize that all questions are important (even though we may not have time to get to them all)? Here are some ideas:

- Students work in pairs to brainstorm questions, which they write in their lab notebooks. Each pair shares its favorite question or questions.

- In small groups or as a whole class, students write questions on sticky notes and then put them on a piece of chart paper. The class then groups them into categories.

- Each student brainstorms his or her own questions. Then, working in small groups, students create shared documents that include all the questions. The groups organize their questions into categories.

- The teacher creates a question wall or wonder board in the classroom. As questions come up, the teacher encourages students to record them there. This is particularly valuable for questions that cannot be explored in class but that students may be interested in researching on their own.

During a unit, we like to keep track of all student questions because we never know when they might be useful. They can help us drive student-created stories of all types, allow us to connect back to student questions when we're talking about a topic, create extensions based on student questions, or give students chances to explore their questions outside of the classroom.

Using Model Stories to Inspire Deep Thinking and Effective Storytelling

> The universe is made of stories,
> not of atoms.
>
> —Muriel Rukeyser,
> *The Speed of Darkness*

A Story from Melissa

When I first started to teach the sixth-grade unit on the brain and nervous system over ten years ago, I did not know much about the brain. For the first year or two I followed the unit plan diligently. I ran the students through the lessons, quizzed them periodically on vocabulary terms, and then gave them a sheep's brain to dissect as the culminating unit activity. Many admitted afterward that while the dissection was indeed cool, the experience had been rather anticlimactic and did not teach them anything new. I realized that something was missing: context. Without a story to connect to the experience, it was just an activity and had little meaning.

Then, on a visit to the Harvard Anatomical Museum, I discovered the skull of Phineas Gage. While he was working on a railroad construction project in the late 1840s, a thirteen-pound tamping iron pierced his skull during an explosion.

He survived but started to develop personality changes, and he became the subject of many medical studies. I was fascinated. This was the gripping story that I needed to provide the context for my students!

Now I read *Phineas Gage: A Gruesome but True Story About Brain Science*, by John Fleischman (2002), to students at the beginning of the brain unit. Students are totally entranced and can't wait to learn more. The story provides them with a genuine sense of purpose for learning about how the brain works and what happens when it doesn't work the way we hope or expect it to.

I also use the book to point out the features of effective science stories. Fleischman's book reads like fiction—it has a bewitching plot, a magnetic main character, and it is written in a voice and tone that make it hard to put down. The details Fleischman provides enthrall readers so they are highly motivated to find out what happens to Phineas.

The story of Phineas Gage is a terrific example of what we call a *model story* (in literacy these are often referred to as *mentor texts*). We weave these into science instruction to deepen thinking and help students craft their own science stories. Our ultimate goal is to have our students find their own writing style to frame their science understanding in the context of a compelling story that captivates the audience like Paul Fleischman does.

What Are Model Stories and Why Use Them?

Model stories can take many forms: books, journals, magazines, newspaper articles, and other types of media with strong elements of story, such as videos, podcasts, speeches, TED talks, online presentations (such as Prezis), and infographics.

We choose the type of model story depending on the content we're teaching, the audience, and our purpose. Our goals for using model stories may be to engage students in the topic, deepen their thinking, or showcase the features of effective stories.

Model Stories Engage Students and Deepen Their Thinking

Picture yourself reading aloud to your students, circled up in chairs. You've chosen an engaging, well-written, challenging text you know will captivate their imaginations. You pause at key points to ask students to visualize, recall, wonder, infer, and predict—moves that help the students who might not otherwise be able to access the text independently to make connections. Ultimately, these pauses invite all of your students to think more deeply about the ideas being presented. The ideas you are asking about are central to the unit you are teaching, even if the students don't know it yet. The experience and the model story launch student thinking that will be threaded throughout the unit.

This type of interactive storytelling experience (which can be done with articles, videos, and podcasts as well as books) has many benefits for students. It allows them to

- wonder and ask their own questions
- share their thoughts and questions with their fellow students
- engage with phenomena that cannot be re-created in a classroom
- ponder highly abstract ideas (e.g., atoms, plate tectonics, DNA transcription)
- connect new information to what they already know and to their own lives and the larger world around them
- appreciate the history of science and the idea of science as a human endeavor
- practice listening closely
- think critically and evaluate information presented

Students are invited to actively engage with the story, allowing them to practice scientific habits of mind, think and act like scientists, and share ideas to arrive at collective understanding or perhaps divergent paths of thought that require further exploration. This kind of thinking aloud also allows us to find out what students know about a topic and where they have misconceptions. In order for interactive storytelling to be successful, we plan carefully, thinking about our purpose and choosing a model story that fits our science big ideas. More details about planning for interactive storytelling experiences and an example planning sheet are provided in Lesson 1 on page 43.

Model Stories Show Students How to Create Their Own Powerful Stories

People learn to tell and write mesmerizing stories by listening to good storytellers and reading good stories. When we model the alluring features of stories by using them in instruction and explicitly work with students to decipher how those features are used, we're giving them the tools they need to compose their own captivating science stories.

For example, as a starting point for an eighth-grade exploration of chemistry, we use two pages from Bill Bryson's chapter "The Mighty Atom" in *A Short History of Nearly Everything* (2004). Bryson explores the vast, uncountable number of atoms and their fantastically small size, how atoms are endlessly recycled, the structure of atoms and how atoms are mostly made up of empty space. Students are on the edges of their seats as we read Bryson's masterful analogies that connect the abstractness of atoms to things they recognize; for example, "As Cropper has put it, if an atom were expanded to the size of a cathedral, the nucleus would be only about the size of a fly—but a fly many thousands of times heavier than the cathedral" (141).

In discussions, we point out Bryson's effective use of features such as attention-grabbing hooks, organizational structure, and voice as well as his ability to engage his audience. Students illustrate and explain one of the big ideas from the book (one example follows), then share their stories with each other, and discuss and comment on each other's ideas. As a result, students' own writing pieces become model stories for each other!

The Mighty Atom

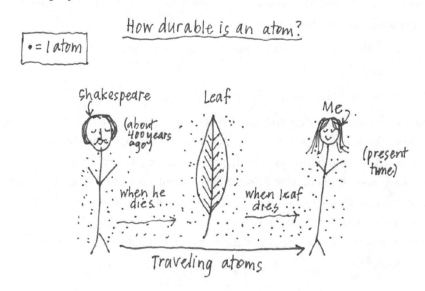

Figure 4.1 Illustration for "The Mighty Atom"

Isn't it weird to think that someone from hundreds of years ago could have had the same exact atoms that are a part of you right now?! Atoms are incredibly durable. People do not even know the exact number of years that atoms last because its [*sic*] so ridiculously high! I found this topic most interesting because it struck me how we are reincarnations. Shakespeares [*sic*] atoms could be a part of us RIGHT NOW and we wouldn't even know! Or perhaps were [*sic*] part of a plant that died a long time ago . . . we still may never know! This goes to show how long atoms live. When creating my drawing I wanted to convey how something so long ago can pass on it's [*sic*] atoms into something new, and whenever that thing passes on, the atoms may come to us, and when we die those atoms will still continue their journey. We die, but atoms keep on persisting!

How Do We Choose Model Stories?

How do we select resources that will inspire students to jump into the stories of science and can teach students how to craft their own stories? (A dirty little secret: it's almost never the textbook.) We consider the following questions when deciding whether or not something would make an effective model story:

- Is the topic engaging?
- Does it target the big ideas that are the focus of the lesson or unit?
- Does the story flow logically?
- Is the story rich and well-crafted? (In other words, does it contain enough of the elements of a good story described in Chapter 2?)
- Is the science accurate?
- Are there moments in the story that could serve as stopping points for student reflection, wonder, and connection?
- Are there key words or concepts that will need to be defined or highlighted?
- Are there illustrations or other visual features that can aid diverse learners' understanding or that might confuse or mislead them?
- What image will students be left with about science or scientists?

Lists of outstanding model story resources (and why we think they're so great) can be found in Appendix B.

Lessons for Using Model Stories with Students

In this section, we provide two lessons for using model stories with students:

Lesson 1: Modeling Good Storytelling and Deepening Thinking

Lesson 2: Using Model Stories to Identify the Features of Strong Science Stories

Lesson 1: Modeling Good Storytelling and Deepening Thinking

Focus Question: How can we model good storytelling and use stories to engage our audience and deepen their thinking?

Big Idea: A good science story can make us think deeply about a topic and spark many questions that we want to learn more about.

Learning Goals: Students will experience a well-told story and learn how effective it can be to engage the audience, spark questions, and deepen thinking.

Materials:

- A model story (text, article, video, podcast, etc.) that fits with the topic you are teaching
- A completed interactive storytelling planning sheet (See the example in Figure 4.3.)
- A collage of images that relate to the model story (optional)

Recommended Time: One fifty-minute session

Notes: If your purpose is to uncover students' initial ideas about a topic or to spark their interest, you might consider using a model story early in the unit. If your goal is to help students synthesize or apply the learning they have already engaged in, then you might use the story later in the unit.

PLANNING FOR STORYTELLING

When we plan for interactive storytelling, we use a planning sheet that outlines our purpose and the actions we'll take (see Figure 4.3 for an example). You can use this tool to do the following:

- *Identify the big ideas:* What is your purpose for doing interactive storytelling at this time? What are the big idea(s) (science, engineering, or nature of science) that you want to showcase?

- *Choose the focus question(s):* What open-ended question(s) do you want students to focus on? What is your purpose for using this story?

- *Get familiar with the story:* Read, watch, or listen to the model story several times. Pay attention to what you are thinking and wondering. Then imagine you are a student in your class. Where might your attention be grabbed? What questions might you have? What parts of the story might you relate to? Jot down your notes.

- *Plan the stopping points:* Where will you strategically stop during the story to invite student thinking and sharing? Identify critical points in the story that will, with the right question, spark discussion and encourage your students to generate ideas, make connections, and take risks with their thinking. Also earmark passages that will likely elicit an emotional response from the students or that might uncover potential misconceptions. Brainstorm a list of potential questions and then jot your best ones down on sticky notes and place them in the text (or in notes) for easy access during storytelling. It's important to carefully consider the number of stopping points. Stopping too often might hinder the flow of the story, and stopping too infrequently could miss opportunities to engage the students.

- *Craft a question to ask before the story begins:* Formulate an engaging or intriguing question to ask before launching the story that frames one of the big ideas you hope students will take away from the experience. This warms up students before getting into the story and primes their minds for the experience. For instance, before reading *Into the Deep: The Life of Explorer and Naturalist William Beebe* (Sheldon 2009), we ask: "If you could have your passion become your profession, what might it be?"

- *Decide how students will share their thinking:* Each time you stop and pose a question, you invite students to actively engage with the ideas in the story and get in touch with their own thoughts. It's important to give students chances to organize and rehearse their thinking before sharing their ideas in the larger group. For instance, you might have them turn and talk (sometimes referred to as think-pair-share) or ask them to think to themselves for ten to thirty seconds and record their thoughts in their notebooks. We use these techniques when we ask deeper questions that may require students to ponder a bit or questions that may stretch their knowledge (thinking with a partner can help make this less daunting). Vary the ways that students share and interact with ideas during an interactive storytelling session.

- *Create a sheet of mystery images:* In some instances, we like to put together a collage or collection of images related to the big ideas of the story (see Figure 4.2). These images are meant to be mysterious and intriguing. You can pass the sheet around to students before the story begins and ask, "What do you think these images have in common?" or "How do you think these images might relate to the story?"

- *Identify key vocabulary:* Make note of words that students may not be familiar with so you can ask students to explain them or define the terms for them. If there are many words that students might not be familiar with, you may want to preview the most important terms prior to reading to avoid disrupting the interactive experience too much.

Figure 4.2 Mystery photo collage for *The Boy Who Harnessed the Wind* storytelling

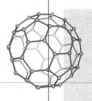

Questions to Ask During an Interactive Storytelling Experience

- Why do you think the author/speaker/videographer chose to include this part/information?

- Why do you think the author/speaker/videographer chose to tell this part this way?

- What effect does this part of the story have on you?

- What questions does this bring up for you?

- What new term did you hear in this passage? What do you think it means?

- How does this section connect to what we have been learning about in class?

- What connections can you make to your own life?

- How did the author/speaker/videographer help you to understand the big idea?

- How did the author/speaker help you make a movie in your mind's eye?

- What kinds of figurative language did the author use?

- What are some reasons _____ might happen?

- Have you ever _____ ?

- What are some other examples from science that illustrate _____ ?

- What do you predict will happen next?

- How does this illustration work to help you understand the story/the science?

- What might someone find confusing about this passage/illustration and why?

- What are you thinking now? [This question is terrific for leaving the conversation wide open to a range of ideas from the students.]

These questions are general, but you can tailor them more specifically to the content of the particular story you're sharing with students.

Lesson:

1. Create an inviting environment for listening and discussion by setting up a circle of chairs with no desks in between or having students sit on the floor in a circle. Make sure all students can see each other.

2. Pose the focus question to the group and ask your prereading question. You could also show a mystery photo collage (see Figure 4.2) and ask students how they think the images might be connected to the story.

3. Read, watch, or listen to the story, stopping at the points you have identified to ask questions and invite student thinking, sharing, and questions.

4. Once students have shared a variety of answers and perspectives, look for opportunities to summarize and deepen student thinking. This is a chance for us to model language to help students find just the right words ("So, I think what you were talking about was . . ."); to name what they are doing ("It sounds like people are inferring . . ."); to assist with any technical terminology and to preview vocabulary students will be seeing during the unit ("The word scientists use for that is . . .").

5. Listen in on some of the student conversations during turn-and-talks if possible. Eavesdropping on these conversations will allow you to later say, for example, "As I listened to the discussion Ryan and Susan were having, I heard a couple of interesting ideas surface . . . ," and then ask a follow-up question of those students to extend the group conversation.

6. Take advantage of openings to extend the discussion and get students to say more. "You mentioned _____; can you tell us more about that?" "Who else can add something to this?" "What are you wondering now, after you shared some of your own thoughts and heard from your fellow scientists?"

INTERACTIVE STORYTELLING PLAN

Grade: Eighth Grade
Unit/Lesson: Energy
Date: September 13, 2015
Title and Author: *The Boy Who Harnessed the Wind,* by William Kamkwamba and Bryan Mealer (2012)

What is the purpose for using this story for an interactive storytelling experience?

- Engage student interest in how energy from the wind can be transformed into other types of energy that can do useful work, like light a light bulb, power a radio, or draw water for crops.

continues

- Inform students about the way that scientists and engineers use their creativity, materials at hand, and science to solve real-world problems.
- Inspire students to dream of one day being able to change their world through science and engineering.

Why choose this story? What makes it worthwhile to share with students? (Text features, student engagement, illustrations/visuals, topic, language/vocabulary, etc.)

The story is inspiring, the text is lovely, the illustrations are captivating, and the message is universal.

What will students be doing before and after the interactive storytelling experience? Where will it be used in the lesson/unit?

Following exploration of electrical circuits, this story will be used to engage students and set the stage for learning about how wind energy (and other energy from motion) can be used to generate electricity for many purposes.

What science/engineering and/or nature of science big ideas are you focusing on?

Nature of Science Big Ideas

- Scientists and engineers are curious and learn by asking questions and exploring different ways to answer them.
- Scientists and engineers gather evidence to answer their questions in many ways (observing, investigating, seeking information from reliable sources).
- Scientists and engineers make claims based on their evidence.
- Scientists and engineers share their claims and evidence with others (who may or may not agree with their findings).
- The most important tools of scientists and engineers are their minds, imaginations, and creativity. However, they often use tools and technology to obtain more information than they can gather with their senses.

Energy Big Ideas

- Energy can be moved from place to place by moving objects or through sound, light, or electric currents.
- Energy can be transferred from place to place by electric currents, which can then be used to produce motion, sound, heat, or light. The currents may have been produced to begin with by transforming the energy of motion into electrical energy.

Focus question(s) for the interactive storytelling experience:

- How do scientists and engineers use their creativity, materials at hand, and science to solve real-world problems?
- How is energy transferred from one form to another?

BEFORE INTERACTIVE STORYTELLING

Possible question to ask before reading to get students to start thinking about the big idea:

- Can you identify a machine that has transformed the world? Why was it so important?

Focus question to share with students before reading:

- How do scientists and engineers use their creativity, materials at hand, and science to solve real-world problems?

DURING INTERACTIVE STORYTELLING

Stopping Point	Teaching Move and Purpose
First stopping point: "In a small village in Malawi, where people had no money for lights." (2)	Turn-and-talk: What do you think this means: "where people had no money for lights"? (Invites students to think about the conditions that people in Malawi live in.)
Second stopping point: "How does its engine make it go?" (6)	Whole-group discussion: What kind of boy is William, and how do you know? (Surfaces ideas about the characteristics of scientists and engineers.)
Third stopping point: "Slowly he built the sentence: 'Windmills can produce electricity and pump water.' He closed his eyes and saw a windmill outside his home, pulling electricity from the breeze and bringing light to the dark valley." (11–12)	Turn-and-talk: What happened when William went to the library? How did this experience affect him? Have you ever had an experience like that? (Connects the story to students' lives and experiences.)
Fourth stopping point: "I will build electric wind." (14)	Whole-group discussion: What does William mean when he says: "I will build electric wind"? (Prompts thinking about how engineers solve problems.)
Fifth stopping point: "This boy is *misala*. Only crazy people play with trash!" (15)	Turn-and-talk: People thought that the things William found in the junkyard were trash. Do you agree? Why or why not? (Makes a connection to the reuse of materials and how a junkyard can be a treasure trove in an underdeveloped country.)

continues

Sixth stopping point: "With sore hands once slowed by hunger and darkness, William connected wires to a small bulb, which flickered at first, then surged as bright as the sun." (23)	Whole-group discussion: Did you do something like this in our electricity lesson? How is what William did similar to what you did? [He connected wires to a light bulb and made it light. Students did this using a battery as an energy source.] What did William use as the energy source? (Formative assessment to see if students can connect their previous experience to William's design.)
Seventh stopping point: "Electric wind can feed my country. . . . And that was the strongest magic of all." (26)	Turn-and-talk: What does William mean when he says this? How can wind feed a country? (Invites students to think about how renewable energy sources can help people survive.)

AFTER INTERACTIVE STORYTELLING

Wrapping up and reflecting on the big idea(s): What will you say to guide students to pull their ideas together to support the big idea?

Ask students: "What characteristics did William have that allowed him to do something that changed his world? Do you have those characteristics? What makes you think that?"

Read the excerpt from the back of the book: "The true story of a boy whose great idea and perseverance lit up his home and inspired the world." Ask, "What does it mean to persevere? How did William persevere?"

If time allows, read the two biographical pages that follow the story *or* have students read it for homework (and gather additional information from William's website: www.williamkamkwamba.com).

Ask: "If you could choose a real-world problem to solve, what would it be? Why? What steps would you take to solve the problem?" (This could also be a homework writing assignment.)

Optional: Show students the eight-minute documentary about William on his website so they can hear the story in his own words (http://movingwindmills.org/documentary).

Figure 4.3 Putting interactive storytelling into action with *The Boy Who Harnessed the Wind*

Lesson 2: Using Model Stories to Identify the Features of Strong Science Stories

Focus Question: What makes a science story powerful? What are the features that need to be included?

Big Idea: In order to craft good science stories, we need to know what the key elements are and be able to identify them in other people's stories.

Learning Goals: Students will identify the features of effective science stories using model stories.

Materials:

- A model story (text, article, video, podcast, and so on) that fits with the topic you are teaching and meets the criteria for powerful model stories
- Sticky notes, chart paper, and markers

Recommended Time: Two to three fifty-minute sessions

Note: Prior to this lesson, students should be exposed to a number of interactive storytelling experiences.

Lesson:

1. Based on their experiences so far, ask students to identify what features they think powerful science stories have. Students should do this preassessment individually and then turn and talk. We often have students record their thoughts on sticky notes and post them on chart paper. When they have placed their sticky notes on the chart paper, read through them and ask students how they could "chunk" or categorize the notes. You will end up with a Features of Powerful Stories chart that looks something like the one pictured in Figure 4.4.

2. Explain that the class will be looking at an array of model science stories to see if there are any other features that are important. Then facilitate an interactive storytelling experience using a text you've used before. This time around, instead of focusing on science content or practices, hone in on the features of the story. Stop and ask questions like the ones outlined in the text box on page 53. Repeat this process with three to four different types of stories (books, articles, videos, podcasts, and so on) during this lesson. Each time, as students discover new features of effective stories, add them to your Features of Powerful Stories chart, guiding students toward any features that might be missing. See Figure 2.2 on pages 19–20 for a full list of features.

3. Have students create anchor charts (such as the one shown in Figure 4.5) to show examples of the ingredients of powerful science stories (taken from one of the stories that the students analyzed).

Figure 4.4 Students brainstorm what they think features of powerful science stories are and then, as a class, we chunk them into groups to create our list of criteria.

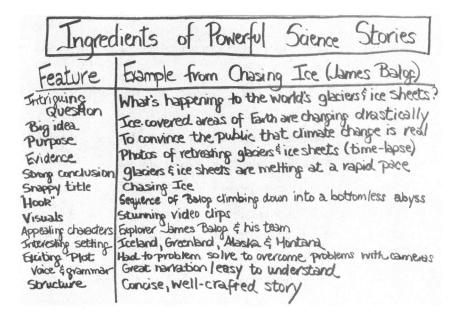

Ingredients of Powerful Science Stories

Feature	Example from Chasing Ice (James Balog)
Intriguing Question	What's happening to the world's glaciers & ice sheets?
Big idea	Ice-covered areas of Earth are changing drastically
Purpose	To convince the public that climate change is real
Evidence	Photos of retreating glaciers & ice sheets (time-lapse)
Strong conclusion	glaciers & ice sheets are melting at a rapid pace
Snappy title	Chasing Ice
"Hook"	Sequence of Balog climbing down into a bottomless abyss
Visuals	Stunning video clips
Appealing characters	Explorer James Balog & his team
Interesting setting	Iceland, Greenland, Alaska & Montana
Exciting Plot	Had to problem solve to overcome problems with cameras
Voice & grammar	Great narration / easy to understand
Structure	Concise, well-crafted story

Figure 4.5 Class- or student-created charts can be posted in the classroom or on class websites to help students as they craft their own stories.

Questions to Help Students Identify the Features of Effective Science Stories

- What makes this story memorable for you?

- What is the question or problem that the author is seeking to answer?

- Is there a message to the story? What is it? How can you tell?

- Tell me about the ending of the story. Is it effective? Why or why not?

- Does the author provide evidence to explain the story?

- What is it about the story that makes it feel relevant and interesting to you?

- When was your interest first grabbed? When did you say to yourself, *I'm really interested in finding out more!?*

continues

- Were there any features of the story that helped you understand the story's message and clarify the science?

- Can you describe the characters in the story? Were they interesting? Could you relate to them?

- Did the setting of the story impact your interest or ideas about the story?

- Could you follow the flow of the story? Why or why not?

- Was there a plot? Did it seem interesting or kind of flat?

- Tell me about the voice and tone of the story. Did you feel that it was written in a manner that made it easy for you to understand? Why or why not?

- How did the author help you understand the science content?

Identifying Purpose, Audience, and Setting to Choose Storytelling Tools

5

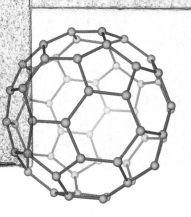

Great stories happen to those who can tell them.

—Ira Glass

A Story from Janet

"Death by PowerPoint." I'm sure you've heard this phrase and have many vivid memories to personally illustrate it. I know I do. At a recent conference, I was sitting in a crowded, warm room (after lunch), listening to a speaker read his plain-vanilla slides word for word using acronyms and language that I didn't understand. My eyes were drooping uncontrollably and I tried to pinch myself to stay awake. All I could think was, *When will it end?* The speaker may have had an amazing story to tell, but the message was lost because of the way he was communicating it.

Before students craft different types of science stories, they need to think carefully about what the purpose of their story is, who will be reading, watching, or listening to it, and how they will communicate it. It doesn't do anyone any good to craft a story that no one can understand or wants to engage with! For instance, if a high school student wants to teach first graders about recycling, will a thirty-minute PowerPoint be effective? Probably not. It would be much better to create a picture book, a short video with engaging visuals, or even a live skit.

Factors That Inform How We Tell a Story

Students need to consider three things when planning how to communicate a story effectively:

1. The purpose (What question does the story focus on? What do we want the audience to walk away with?)

2. The audience (Who is in the audience and what is their background knowledge?)

3. The setting and any related constraints (Where and how will the story be delivered? Will it be told in person? Online? In print?)

Purpose

Students often lose sight of the purpose when they are creating a story. Here are some possible purposes for student science stories:

- to share an explanation with others and try to convince them that it is the best one to answer a question or to encourage others to take action (explanatory stories)

- to outline what scientists have learned about a specific topic, teach or inform others, or entice others to take action (such as cleaning up a local river) (informational stories)

- to tell about the discoveries, struggles, and personal details of scientists (including themselves) (personal stories)

In addition, for all types of science stories, an overarching purpose can be sharing enthusiasm and excitement about science and a sense of wonder about the world.

When students begin to create science stories, we ask them, "What do you think the purpose of this story should be?" and "Why are you creating it?" In many cases, we identify the purpose for students, but they still need to be crystal clear on what it is.

After students become familiar with thinking in terms of the purpose of their stories, you can provide them with opportunities to choose the purpose for themselves. For example, if students are curious about a certain topic, you might let them research and create a story to answer a question that is of particular interest. Why not let them choose their purpose too? It may be helpful to brainstorm a list of possible purposes with students (and when they would be appropriate). This list will help them choose the purpose they think best fits their story.

Audience

Knowing and tailoring the story appropriately for the audience is vital. For example, consider a situation in which high school students are creating stories about an experiment they did with model rockets. When communicating with their peers, they might use language like *projectile motion*, *vectors*, and *gravitational force*, and their visuals might include complex graphs of data they collected. However, if the audience were a class of first graders, the language and explanations would be much simpler. Their visuals should also be very basic and appealing to young children.

Often, the only audience for student stories is the teacher (since the teacher is typically using the stories to assess student understanding). With such a limited audience, students don't get a chance to practice what people do in real life: communicate effectively to a wide range of audiences. So whenever possible, we try to set up situations in which students share their stories with authentic audiences. We all learn best when we have to teach something to others. In addition, we find that when there is an authentic audience, students have higher expectations for themselves. After all, who wants his or her blog post (which will be read by parents and others from around the world) to include grammatical and spelling errors?

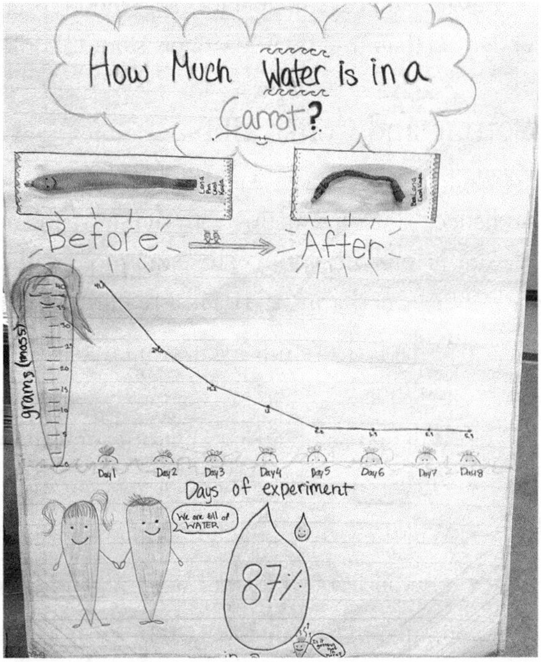

When we work with students to help them characterize their audience prior to crafting their stories, we ask them what they think is important to know about their audience. From this, we create a class list of questions that are helpful to think about, such as these:

Figure 5.1 We asked these sixth graders to present their results on how much water is in a carrot in a way that all children in the school (including kindergartners) would understand. What do you think? Did they do a good job of considering their audience?

- How much does the audience already know about the topic?
- What does the audience need to know in order understand the story? Why does the audience need to know it?

- What is your relationship to the audience? (to determine tone)

- Is the audience likely to agree or disagree with you? Might some people in the audience have a strong negative reaction? If so, why?

- What will the audience do with the information from your story?

The answers to these questions help us figure out what information to include, how to present the story (including visuals), how to organize the information, and the level of detail and vocabulary required (based on the existing knowledge of the audience).

Lesson 1 on page 60 includes suggestions on teaching students how differences in the audience (and the purpose) impact how stories should be told.

Setting and Constraints

In addition to the purpose and audience, students need to think about the setting, how the audience will be interacting with the story, and any constraints before they choose the appropriate way to tell their stories. These questions will help students make effective choices, particularly if they are sharing stories in a nonprint format:

- What is the setting? Will you be sharing your story in print, in person, or remotely (online)?

- Will people be sitting, standing, or walking around?

- Do you need to be there, or can you walk away and have the story present itself?

- Will the setting be loud? Will other distracting things be happening nearby?

- Do you want feedback from your audience?

As outlined in Lesson 2 (page 64), when working with students to make sure their stories are communicated effectively, we have them answer these questions first before they choose an appropriate storytelling tool. When students are considering these questions, it might be helpful for them to share their settings with others to get their feedback on what type of storytelling tool might work best in specific situations. In this exercise, they need to visualize the setting (and describe it in detail) so that they can think through how their storytelling tool might work in that setting. They can describe it orally or they might even want to draw a sketch.

Student Choice

If possible, we feel that it's really important to allow students to choose the best way to tell their stories. Lesson 2 (page 64) outlines a strategy for teaching students how to choose appropriate storytelling tools by themselves.

However, sometimes we may want all students to communicate their stories in the same form based on what we want them to be doing or thinking (giving feedback to each other, sharing with a global audience, and so on). In these instances, be transparent about why you've chosen the storytelling tool for a certain project. This is a great way to model the thinking process of how to match the tool to the purpose, audience, and setting.

Tools for Storytelling

There are a multitude of innovative and engaging ways for students to share their science stories: written stories, videos, digital stories, podcasts, posters, photo-essays, comic strips, and more. To think of this through a scientific lens, we're looking at the age-old overarching science theme of form and function: what is the best form for your story, given your purpose, audience, and setting?

After we introduce students to the concepts of purpose, audience, and setting, we often have them look at and listen to a variety of science stories. As they do this, students identify each story's purpose, audience, and possible setting(s). They also think about why the author may have chosen that particular storytelling tool (and what other tools might have worked just as successfully). By charting out the various purposes, audiences, and settings for the stories, students begin to get a sense of what types of tools match different situations.

Building on what they have just learned, we then brainstorm a chart on various storytelling tools that match a variety of purposes (see Figure 5.2). This class chart will become an essential tool for students when they choose storytelling tools on their own.

If your purpose is to . . .	You might consider . . .
Interact in person with the audience	A live presentation with an easy-to-use slide show, such as Google Slides or PowerPoint
Give the viewer choices about how to make connections in a different order, or to focus on one part of the story	A nonlinear presentation, such as Prezi
Share stories with a global audience on the web	A presentation in which you can record your voice (podcast) and include video or images (e.g., Prezi or Explain Everything)

continues

If your purpose is to . . .	You might consider . . .
Share with a wide audience and give and receive feedback	A podcast published through a blogging-type website
Encourage peer-to-peer discussion that deepens student thinking about a topic	Blog discussions or in-class discussions
Share projects informally in a large room with many participants	A poster
Communicate with a wide audience in an easily accessible format that does not require use of online media	Print material
Present key information visually to catch the attention of a wide range of people (either on the Internet or in person)	An infographic, a comic strip, or a compelling graph or data table

Figure 5.2 The class generates a chart to help students match their purposes with the appropriate storytelling tools.

Lessons for Teaching Students How to Choose Storytelling Tools

In this section, we provide two lessons for teaching students to choose effective storytelling tools:

- Lesson 1: Matching Storytelling Tools to Purpose, Audience and Setting
- Lesson 2: Telling an Effective Story

These lessons can be used with any type of science story.

Lesson 1: Matching Storytelling Tools to Purpose, Audience, and Setting

Focus Question: How do authors choose the best storytelling tools to tell their stories?

Big Idea: An effective science story is communicated in a way that matches its purpose, audience, and setting.

Learning Goals: Students will learn about the various types of storytelling tools and analyze examples to determine how they can choose a tool to match a story's purpose, audience, and setting.

Materials:

- Model stories of many different types (texts, articles, charts and graphs, picture books, videos, digital stories, podcasts, photo-essays, graphic novels, etc.) (See lists of model stories in Appendix B for ideas.)
- Storytelling Tool Cards (see Figure 5.4)
- Chart paper and markers

Recommended Time: One to two fifty-minute sessions

Lesson:

Analyzing Different Types of Storytelling Tools

1. Ask students: "What different ways do you think science stories can be communicated?" (You may get answers like books, articles, videos, podcasts, photographs, tables, and graphs.) Create a "Storytelling Tools" chart to compile student ideas. (You can add to this list throughout the lesson.) Explain that students will be looking at these different storytelling tools in depth to determine how authors choose the best storytelling tools to tell their stories.

2. Have students write a response to the question, "How do you think authors choose what tool to use to tell their stories? What do they consider?" Have students share ideas. (*Note:* This can be used as a formative assessment. Based on their responses, you can tell what ideas you may need to guide them toward).

3. Tell students that they will be looking at and listening to a variety of science stories. Their task will be to record what they think the purpose of each story is, who the target audience is, what setting this type of story would work in, why they think the author chose that storytelling tool, and reasons for their answers. In small groups or pairs, have students read, look at, or listen to and respond to at least three different types of science stories. We suggest giving each group different science stories. Using a wider array of stories leads to richer discussions and exposure to a diverse collection of situations. (If groups finish early, ask them to think about what other storytelling tools might work for the author's purpose and audience.)

4. After students finish, ask them to share their findings with another group; then have students share as a whole group. Students could create charts in their groups like the one shown in Figure 5.3. In turn, this information could be combined into a class chart.

group 1

Science Storytelling Analysis

Story/Tool	Purpose	Audience	Setting	Why This Tool?
Seeds Saved Dinosaur-birds from extinction (podcast)	Share new fact research explanation	general public	online	Share with wide audience (globally) Easy to listen when travelling or doing other tasks
The weird, wonderful world of bioluminescence (TED Talk)	Teach Get people excited about science	general public	online	Share with wide audience (globally) Visually appealing Engaging
Create a bird habitat (Infographic)	Teach Convince people to take action	Children	online	Share with wide audience (globally) Easy to read great visuals

Figure 5.3 Students analyze science stories to find out the relationship between storytelling tools, purpose, audience, and setting.

5. Building on what they have just learned, create a class chart of storytelling tools (see example in Figure 5.2). In addition to the tools used in the science stories that the groups worked with, this list should include the tools that students brainstormed in step 1.

Matching Storytelling Tools to Purpose and Audience

1. Tell students that now they'll get a chance to choose storytelling tools to match different story purposes and audiences. They'll also have to explain why they chose the tools.

2. Choose one of the purpose cards from the Storytelling Tool Cards (see Figure 5.4) and share it with the class. Explain that each small group of two to three students will get different audience and setting cards (randomly shuffled). Each group will choose a type of storytelling tool to match their purpose, audience, and setting and explain why they chose it. Ask groups to share. You can do as many additional rounds of this activity as you feel are necessary. On future rounds, you might choose to hand out different purpose cards to each group.

Purpose: Convince your audience to start a recycling program	**Purpose:** Share your research on the adaptations of different animals	**Purpose:** Inform your audience about a new marine sanctuary
Purpose: Tell the story of Jacques Cousteau and how he impacted the protection of world oceans	**Purpose:** Get feedback on your explanation of how a certain type of landform is created over time	**Purpose:** Share current theories about the landscape and past history of Mars based on what we know about Earth
Purpose: Explain how our thinking about the universe changed over time (and the role of tools in these changes)	**Purpose:** Convince your audience to create a habitat for birds and butterflies	**Purpose:** Present information and encourage discussion about using more sustainable energy sources in your town
Audience: Kindergartners	**Audience:** Fifth graders	**Audience:** Middle school students
Audience: Community members	**Audience:** A global audience	**Audience:** Scientists at a conference
Audience: Town government	**Audience:** Parents	**Audience:** High school students
Setting: Online	**Setting:** An auditorium	**Setting:** Outdoors at a local community fair
Setting: Public meeting	**Setting:** Museum-type exhibit	**Setting:** Poster session (where people are circulating throughout a large hall)
Setting: Science talk in the classroom	**Setting:** Radio broadcast	**Setting:** An outdoor camp

Figure 5.4 Storytelling Tool Cards (reproducible found at www.heinemann.com/products/E08677.aspx)

Lesson 2: Telling an Effective Story

Focus Question: How can we effectively communicate our science stories?

Big Idea: An effective science story is communicated in a way that matches its purpose, audience, and setting.

Learning Goal: Students will learn how to choose good storytelling tools to tell their stories.

Materials:

- Access to storytelling tools
- "Storytelling Tools" chart (created in Lesson 1)
- Copies of a blank "Storytelling Tool Evaluation" chart (see completed example in Figure 5.5)

Recommended Time: One to two fifty-minute sessions

Notes: Prior to this lesson, students should identify a question for their science story (if it's informational or personal). For an explanation, they should do a hands-on investigation and gather their data.

Lesson:

1. Explain that students will be planning how to communicate their stories to a target audience in a certain setting. Ask students to respond to the following questions in their notebooks:

   - What's the purpose of your story? What do you want to communicate? What do you want your audience to come away with? Why are you telling this story?
   - Who's your audience? What do you think their background is on this topic (if any)?
   - What's the setting—where will you be? Will you be creating printed material that people will be looking at when you aren't present? Will you be presenting in person or online? If you will be there in person, will people be sitting, standing, or walking around? Do you need to be there, or can you walk away and have the story present itself? What constraints exist (e.g., Will you be at an outside location with no electricity or screen? Will there be loud distractions nearby? Will the audience be coming and going)? Will you need feedback from your audience?

2. Refer back to the "Storytelling Tools" chart from Lesson 1 and talk about which options are available for students to use to communicate their stories. Next, ask them (in small groups or individually) to analyze the storytelling tools to determine which tools would be the best to deliver their stories to their audience in the appropriate setting. Give students a blank "Storytelling Tool Evaluation" chart for this task. (See completed example in Figure 5.5.)

Storytelling Tool Evaluation		
Tool	**Ways This Tool Might Be Effective for My Purpose, Audience, and Setting**	**Possible Drawbacks of This Tool**
Prezi	• Can be visually appealing for the audience • Novel way of presenting information • Engages audience's attention • User can decide to skip over some parts or go in a different order	• User has to click through • Can be unsettling for some viewers because of the zooming feature • Not interactive
Podcast	• Great for auditory learners • Invites the audience to use their imaginations to visualize the story	• Audio only • For some audiences, may need to provide some type of accompanying visuals • Not interactive
Blog	• Can incorporate text, photos, and video to provide multiple ways for the audience to access the story • The audience can provide feedback and comments and participate in an online discussion about the story topic	• If it's open to the public, screening of public comments may be necessary
Infographic	• Presents key information in a visually appealing way • Easy for the audience to see what the key information is at a glance	• Not interactive • Hard to print out if the audience wants to get a hard copy

Figure 5.5 Example "Storytelling Tool Evaluation" chart for a story that students decide to tell online

3. After students choose a storytelling tool based on their analysis, have them exchange feedback with their peers on their tool, focusing on whether the choices of materials and media match the purpose, audience, and setting of the story. Students can use this feedback to make a final decision on their storytelling tool.

6 Explanatory Stories of Science

Humans are natural-born scientists. When we're born, we want to know why the stars shine. We want to know why the sun rises.

—Michio Kaku

A Story from Janet

Growing up in rural Pennsylvania, I spent most of my spare time exploring the woods behind our house. One day, I noticed two different but intertwined sets of tracks in the mud near a stream. What animals made the tracks? Where were they going? Was one animal chasing the other? After observing the tracks closely, I suspected that the larger tracks were made by a fox. The size and shape of the tracks, which were similar to my dog's footprints, seemed to be foxlike. In addition, my father and I had seen a pair of foxes in that area the week before. The smaller tracks looked different and appeared to have small claws. Maybe they were from a squirrel that was being chased by the fox.

As many children do, I was trying to answer my questions and make sense of what I had observed by attempting to tell the story of how the animals might have interacted. At the time, I didn't realize that I was using the same process that scientists have used for centuries as we've strived to explain the unknown and make sense of our world.

Now that I am a science teacher, I realize how important it is to interweave science practices (such as constructing explanations) throughout science content. The authentic process of constructing explanations (like explaining the tracks I found in the forest) is central to what science is and how it works. As a result, the foundational skills of constructing, critiquing, and refining explanations (which are also key literacy skills) should be embedded throughout science instruction at all grade levels.

Why Do Scientists Construct, Critique, and Refine Explanations?

Scientists (and other people) create many different types of stories to explain the fascinating phenomena that we observe around us. Once scientists have identified a question, they make observations and investigate, using the resulting data to craft an explanation to answer the question. Then they engage in the process of discussion, critique, and refinement with other scientists in their quest to find the best explanation to answer the question. The ultimate goal is to create the strongest, best-supported explanation possible—one that will advance our collective understanding of the world. This process of sharing, learning from one another, and questioning the thinking of others is a vital part of how we collectively build understanding in science.

The practices of constructing, critiquing, and refining explanations have occurred throughout the centuries as people have asked questions about what they've observed in the natural world and used what they know to create stories of how our world works. In earliest times, humans relied on myths to make sense of the unexplained. As more sophisticated tools became available, we modified our explanations based on new evidence. This process continues today.

What Does a Scientific Explanation Include?

The practices of constructing, critiquing, and refining explanations are complicated. Many terms (e.g., *argument*, *explanation*, *claims*, *evidence*, and *reasoning*) are used in different ways by various sources. This can be confusing! In this book, we use *constructing explanations* to refer to the process of making claims based on evidence (connected by reasoning).

As shown in Figure 6.1, scientists who construct explanations typically do the following:

1. Ask a question (sparked by observing something novel or unexplained).
2. Make observations using their senses (collect data).
3. Look for patterns in the observations and make inferences based on the patterns they uncover, their previous findings, background knowledge, and judgment.
4. Construct a claim to answer the question based on their observations and inferences.
5. Identify the big idea that connects the claim and evidence; this reasoning is a synthesis of their existing science knowledge and knowledge gained from new observations.

The Difference Between Inferences and Claims

Inferences are very similar to claims. They are statements that are created based on observations using prior knowledge and judgment, but they may not answer the question (like the claim does). In some situations, we need to combine several inferences to create the claim. Figure 6.2 shows the process of constructing an explanation based on the scenario of finding a mystery object on the beach.

Components of a Strong Explanation

A strong explanation has five main components:

1. A q*uestion:* The query that is being investigated.
2. A *claim*: A statement that answers the question based on evidence (observations). The claim reflects patterns noticed in the observations and can be built from a series of inferences (or in some cases from a single inference). (When scientists use their opinion, judgment, or what they already know to answer a question, they are making a claim.)
3. *Relevant, reliable, and sufficient evidence to support the claim*: The specific observations that support the claim. This evidence must be relevant to the claim, reliable (e.g., the results can be repeated), and sufficient (many pieces of evidence should be provided, not just one).
4. *Clear reasoning*: Reasoning that connects the claim and evidence to the big scientific idea, explaining why the claim makes sense based on the evidence. (This may be based on background knowledge or previous results; in some cases, student reasoning may be inaccurate based on prior misconceptions.)
5. *Counterclaims*: Other possible claims that could be made to explain the same results and justification as to why your claim is better.

To get an idea of these components in action, take a look at the following example of a student explanation.

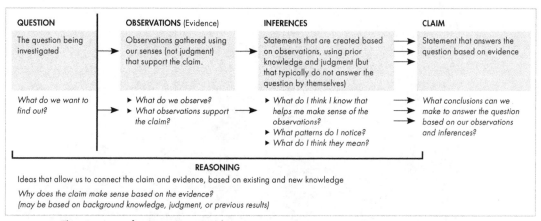

Figure 6.1 The process of constructing explanations

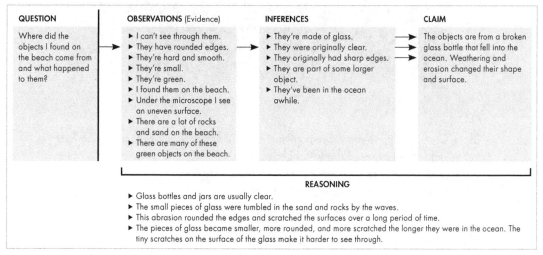

Figure 6.2 Beach mystery objects: An example to illustrate how explanations are constructed

Photosynthesis Experiment

Question: Can photosynthesis occur in the dark?

Claim: Based on my observations, I believe that photosynthesis cannot occur in the dark.

Evidence: Test tubes at beginning of the experiment [see Figure 6.3]
My group observed, that, even if the test tubes had started out as being the same color, after two days, the CL and CD tubes had not changed, while the D tube had darkened very slightly, taking on a greenish tint. The L tube, however, had changed from yellow all the way to blue; the L tube was also the only test tube to have bubbles in it, which were collecting near the top of the test tube.
Test tubes after day 2 [see Figure 6.3]

Reasoning: I believe that my claim is supported by observed and scientific evidence. Bromothymol blue (BTB), as a chemical, turns yellow when carbon dioxide

Figure 6.3 Photo of the experiment after day 2

is released into it; likewise, it returns to blue when the carbon dioxide evaporates into the air, or, in the case of this experiment, is withdrawn through the process of photosynthesis.

Photosynthesis converts carbon dioxide and water into glucose, and, in the process, releases oxygen. I can infer that, because there were oxygen bubbles in the L tube, photosynthesis occurred (the Parafilm prevented oxygen from simply "leaking in"). I can also conclude that, because there was a lack of oxygen bubbles in the D tube, photosynthesis did not occur there.

We can conclude, that, because the L tube turned blue, photosynthesis occurred there. Plants absorb carbon dioxide molecules as part of the photosynthesis process; when the carbon dioxide is removed from the BTB, the color returns to blue. Since the D tube remained yellow (meaning there was still carbon dioxide in the test tube) while the L tube returned back to blue (meaning the plant had absorbed the CO_2), I can infer that photosynthesis didn't occur in the D tube, but did so in the L tube.

In my group's mental model, we are trying to show, through a diagram, the process by what would happen to the Elodea plant when it tried to undergo photosynthesis in both the light and the dark [see Figure 6.4].

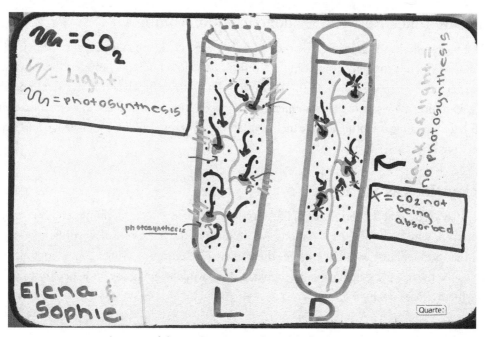

Figure 6.4 Visualization of the students' mental model of what happened in their experiment

Light energy is what powers the process of photosynthesis. When put under a LED light, that energy can be acquired. However, in the dark, the light is harder to come by. As you can see in the model, this lack of light prevents photosynthesis from occurring completely; thus, there is no need for the carbon dioxide to be absorbed, which explains the lack of color change in the D tube.

The experiment tells us that plants cannot photosynthesize very well in the dark; however, it doesn't say very much about whether it can grow in the dark, since the setup of the experiment really shows what effect light (or lack thereof) has on photosynthesis, not on overall plant growth.

In this example, the student was actively engaged in creating and telling the story of what happened and why. She gathered the evidence and then made sense of it by placing it in the context of her broader scientific understanding about photosynthesis. The student used her own data and thinking to answer the question by creating a claim. Her reasoning explained in detail why the evidence supported her claim, using her knowledge of the big scientific ideas and her previous knowledge about photosynthesis. The evidence provided the support for her claim, but the reasoning explained why what was happening made sense. The reasoning is actually the explanation part of the explanation!

The Difference Between Evidence and Reasoning

Sometimes students struggle with the difference between evidence and reasoning. They often repeat the evidence instead of providing reasoning. The close interplay between these two parts of an explanation can contribute to this confusion. Evidence is the data that support the claim, while reasoning allows us to make connections between the claim and the evidence. Reasoning is based on a big scientific idea, which is often based on our previous knowledge and experiences from other investigations.

Explanations as Stories

Some may argue that the term *story* is not appropriate to use when describing scientific explanations. But why can't these explanations, which serve as the backbone of scientific inquiry, be recounted and told in a way that engages the audience? Communicating explanations clearly and succinctly, using the applicable elements of story, while keeping the audience in mind, will make them more convincing.

Lessons for Teaching Students to Craft Strong Explanations

Constructing explanations may be a new skill for most students, so we need to take time to explain why the process is important, define the components, and share plenty of examples. Most importantly, we need to model and scaffold how to construct explanations. Providing students with multiple and varied opportunities to work with explanations over time will be necessary in order for this practice to become part of the way they work and think. Also keep in mind that explanations do not always have to take the form of polished written products; they can be quick-and-dirty short entries in student notebooks or blogs, illustrations or posters, or informal oral presentations in group discussions. We prefer them to be based on data from students' own hands-on investigations, but you can provide data (raw data, tables, graphs, maps, and photographs) from other sources for students to analyze and use as the basis of explanations.

The following lessons follow a sequence (assuming that students are just beginning to construct explanations), but they can be taught in any order depending on your students' needs:

- Lesson 1: Introducing Explanations
- Lesson 2: Constructing Explanations in Small Groups
- Lesson 3: Identifying the Parts of Explanations
- Lesson 4: Analyzing Scientific Explanations Throughout History
- Lesson 5: What Are the Features of a Strong Explanation?
- Lesson 6: Crafting Explanations Based on Our Own Investigation Data
- Lesson 7: Putting the Finishing Touches on Our Explanations
- Lesson 8: Setting the Stage for Critiquing Explanations

Lesson 1: Introducing Explanations

Focus Question: How do scientists use their observations and what they already know about the world to answer their questions and explain their findings?

Big Ideas:

- Observations are made using only our senses (or tools used to extend these senses). They do not include judgment or opinion.
- Scientists use their observations and what they already know to construct explanations in order to answer questions.
- An explanation consists of a claim, evidence that supports the claim, and reasoning (the scientific big ideas and prior knowledge that connect the claims and evidence).
- A claim is typically built based on many inferences (statements that are created based on observations, using prior knowledge and judgment, but that often do not answer the question by themselves).

Learning Goal: Students will learn how scientific explanations are constructed and the parts of an explanation.

Materials:

- Intriguing objects, photographs, videos, or demonstrations
- Chart paper and markers

Recommended Time: One fifty-minute session

Note: The goal of this lesson is to help students distinguish between observations, inferences, and claims made based on those observations and inferences, as well as the reasoning that connects them. This is a difficult concept and may require repeated practice.

Lesson:

1. Share the object, video, or demonstration so that the entire class can see it. Ask: "What do you think this object is? What is this object used for? What happened here?"

2. Share one or two observations of your own with the class. Ask students to make and share observations using only their senses. You may need to help them focus on making observations by asking, "What do you notice?" or "How can you describe what you see without making any judgments?" Record student ideas on a class chart with the headings "Observations," "Inferences," "Claims," and "Reasoning." (Sometimes we just start with an "Observations and Inferences" chart and add the "Claims" and "Reasoning" columns later when we begin talking about those concepts in the lesson.)

3. Clarify for students that when scientists use their opinion, judgment, or what they already know to answer a question, they are making an inference. Model how to make an inference and then encourage students to make inferences about the mystery object, image, or video and record them on the chart. Students may come up with many different inferences for the same set of observations, just as scientists do. They may also use several observations to support a single inference.

4. Guide students to identify the specific observations (evidence) that support each inference. You might circle them and draw arrows to each inference on the chart, using different colors. Students often think that all observations must be used as evidence. Point out that we might not use some observations because they do not support inferences or claims, or we might use them later as our thinking changes.

5. Now ask students, "How can we craft a claim (or maybe several claims) to answer the questions, based on the evidence and our inferences?" (Be sure to tell students that a claim answers the question and may be made up of several inferences.) Add the claims to the chart, connecting the relevant inferences to each claim. To help students stay focused and avoid creative claims (e.g., "aliens landed there and scorched the grass"), it's a good idea to qualify that the claims have to be realistic.

6. Using one of the claims on the chart, ask students: "What prior knowledge do we have that allows us to make this claim based on the evidence?" This is the reasoning. (See next section for a specific example.) Add their ideas for reasoning to the chart.

Putting Lesson 1 into Action in Melissa's Classroom: What Happened Here?

I gave my students the photo in Figure 6.5 and asked: "What do you think happened here?"

Figure 6.5 Mystery photo for Lesson 1

Students worked in small groups to complete an "Observations, Inferences, Claims, and Reasoning" chart. They considered several claims and selected the one they thought they had the most evidence for.

During this activity, students were eager to jump straight to making claims about what they thought had happened in this spot as opposed to starting with what they noticed. I asked them to back up from their possible claims and make a list of observations they could all agree to. I explained that each of their observations could lead them to make smaller inferences and that several of their inferences could lead them to come up with a more conclusive claim. What strikes me when I do this type of activity is how nonlinear it is, even though we have a clear organizer to work with. This reflects the nature of science—in the end, what looks neat and tidy is often the result of a messy process.

OBSERVATIONS

- There is a circular patch with much less grass than the surrounding area.
- There are vines and other plants behind the circular patch.
- There are yellow leaves.
- The grass is a deep green and lush.
- There is a brown barrier that is overgrown with various plants.
- There is a white piece of crumpled trash on the ground.
- There are different types of soil in the grassless patch.

INFERENCES

- It is almost fall.
- The grass is healthy.
- This is not in the middle of nowhere.
- The trash is a crumpled piece of paper.
- The grass/plants are naturally occuring
- Something was on the circular area when the grass was grown.

CLAIMS

- Humans have been to this spot.

- A circular object such as a pool was on the empty patch.

- A camera has been to this spot

Counterclaim:
 - "A rabbit could have eaten the grass," some might say. But we challenge that because rabbits don't eat in a perfect circle.

REASONING

- There is a piece of trash and a man-made barrier.
- A naturally occurring circle is incredibly unlikley.
- An object would've prevented rain fall that made the surrounding grass grow.
- Someone or something had to take the picture that we looked at.

a

Figures 6.6a–b One group's "Observations, Inferences, Claims, and Reasoning" chart along with the claim they thought they had the most evidence for

Based on our observations, we claim that a circular object once occupied this lot and left a dirt patch that lacked the surrounding greenery. Based on the almost perfect circle, we claim that the object that formerly occupied this space was most likely man made (pool) and most likely not a warren of rabbits chewing on the grass, which was our countered theory. We think the object was a pool which would have prevented rainfall and sunlight from getting to the area underneath, therefore, grass wouldn't be able to grow as it did in the surrounding plot. We infer that it's fall based on the yellow leaves on the trees nearby. It makes sense that humans would have taken the pool away as above-ground pools are generally used in the summertime as opposed to the fall because of the change in temperature. Additionally, we believe rabbits (scientifically known as Leporidae) did not eat the grass because this animal does not eat in perfect circles. Overall, we conclude that a pool was likely to have been the inhabitor of the grassless spot and we have strong evidence to support this.

b

Lesson 2: Constructing Explanations in Small Groups

Focus Question: How do scientists use their observations and what they already know about the world to answer their questions?

Big Ideas: Scientists construct explanations to answer questions, based on their observations. An explanation consists of a claim, evidence that supports the claim, and reasoning (the scientific big ideas and prior knowledge that connect the claims and evidence). A claim is typically based on many inferences (statements that are created based on observations using prior knowledge and judgment—but that may not answer the question by themselves).

Learning Goals: Students will review the parts of an explanation and then begin to practice constructing explanations in small groups.

Materials:

- "Constructing Explanations" anchor chart (see example in Figure 6.7)
- Photographs, data from student investigations, or data from other sources (We often start with all students making observations about the same item, but you can also give each group a different one.)
- Chart paper and markers

Recommended Time: Two fifty-minute sessions

Notes: This lesson can be inserted into the curriculum

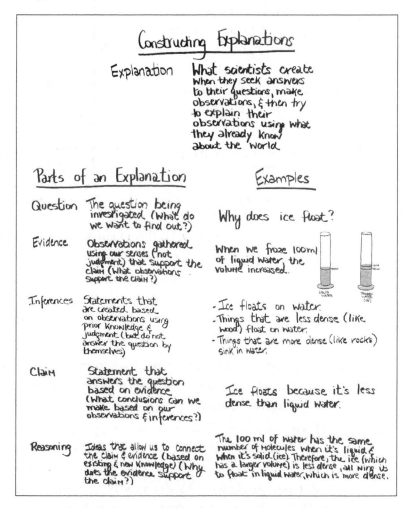

Figure 6.7 Posting clear visuals (like this anchor chart) in the classroom gives students something to easily refer to when they are crafting their own explanations.

where needed to review the elements of scientific explanations. A word wall or anchor chart can help students (including English language learners) remember the components of an explanation.

Lesson:

Day 1

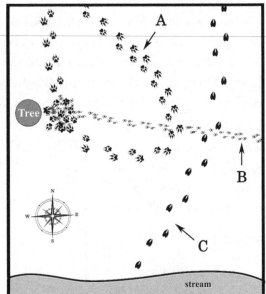

1. Go over the four main parts of a scientific explanation (question, claim, evidence, and reasoning) with students, asking them to share examples from the activity in Lesson 1. Refer to the "Constructing Explanations" anchor chart (which you should make prior to the lesson; see examples in Figure 6.7).

2. Give student groups a photo or data to analyze (see example in Figure 6.8).

3. Explain that student groups will be constructing an explanation to answer a question (in this case, "What

Figure 6.8 Animal track mystery diagram. Focus question: What happened in the forest?

happened in the forest?"). Ask them to make observations and record them on a piece of chart paper with the headings "Observations" and "Inferences."

4. When groups have had a chance to make their observations (about fifteen to twenty minutes), get the whole class together and ask students to share some of their observations. Record these observations on a class chart. This is a good time to clarify with students exactly what a good observation looks like.

5. If necessary, review with students what an inference is. Then ask students to get back into their groups and to make inferences based on their observations (using their prior knowledge and judgment). Have them add these inferences to their group charts.

6. Each group should find one or more observations that supports each inference. They should put the numbers of these supporting observations in parentheses after the inference. If the group can't find an observation to support the inference, remind them that they can always go back and add observations to the first column of their chart. (This step should take about fifteen to twenty minutes.)

Observations	Inferences
1) There are 3 types of tracks.	• At the tree, track A (possibly a wolf) ate track B (possibly a rabbit) after an attack/encounter. (2,5,9,13,16,17)
2) Track A comes up to the tree from the east and then does something and walks away to the north.	• Track C (possibly a deer) came from the stream (4)
3) There's a compass	• Track A (possibly a wolf) was patroling its territory (7,17)
4) Track C is moving north from the stream.	• The tracks were made by animals (8,11,13)
5) Track B goes west to the tree.	• Track C was drinking from the stream. (4)
6) All three tracks cross paths.	• Track C is a deer (8)
7) Track A sort of goes in a loop	• Track B is a rabbit (10,11,16)
8) Track C looks like cloven hooves	• Track A is a wolf (11)
9) Track B stops at the tree	• Track B climbed a tree (13,16,19)
10) Track B is the smallest track.	
11) Tracks A and B both have little toes — looks like paw prints.	
12) There are no tracks in the southwest corner of the image.	
13) Tracks A and B overlap and are pointed in many different directions by the tree.	
14) There is a tree and a stream.	
15) There is a pattern in the tracks that are not by the tree.	
16) Track B extends East or West from the tree.	
17) Track A forms a loop through the area in front of the tree.	

Figure 6.9 Sample "Observations and Inferences" chart for the animal track mystery diagram

Day 2

1. Give the groups a few minutes to review their work from the previous day. Have them choose two to three inferences that they think are very strong and that they'd like to share with the class. Make sure they have at least one observation to support each of these inferences. Add group inferences to a class chart.

2. Review with the class what a claim is. You may want to encourage the students to use the wording "I think [claim] because [evidence]." Remind them that their "Inferences" column is a great place to start constructing their claims.

3. Ask each group to make at least one claim based on their observations, identifying the observations that support the claim. They should write their claim on a second piece of chart paper labeled with the columns "Claims" and "Reasoning." (This will take about ten to fifteen minutes.)

4. Bring the class together and have the groups share some of their claims. Record these on a class chart.

5. Review with students what reasoning is. Ask each group to write at least two to three sentences of reasoning on the chart paper that help explain why their claim makes sense based on the evidence. (This will take about fifteen to twenty minutes.)

Claim: We think that track A (a predator that is possibly a wolf) ate track B (possibly a rabbit). Also, we think that track C is a moose or a deer who was drinking at the stream and then left. We think track A ate track B because track A and track B's footprints intersected at the tree and then track B stopped and track A continued. Also, we think track B is a rabbit because the pawprints are small and light, and track A is a wolf because the pawprints have 4 toes which are pointy. We think track C was drinking at the stream and then left because track C started at the stream and went north across the page, with no apparent interaction with the other animals.

Reasoning: We think that track C is a moose or a deer because the tracks are cloven hooves and they have large strides. Animals with large strides have longer legs, which in turn causes them to be big (like moose and deer). If both track A and track B met at the tree, and only one left, that suggests that the track that didn't leave (track B) could not move because it was hurt or killed. Track A was larger than track B, which usually means that track A is a bigger animal. A lot of the time, bigger animals are predators who eat smaller animals. Track A looked like wolf tracks, and wolves are predators.

Figure 6.10 Sample "Claims and Reasoning" chart for the animal track mystery diagram

6. Display the groups' charts around the room. Have students do a gallery walk for about ten minutes. They should quietly circulate through the classroom, reading the charts

and posting comments and questions using sticky notes. Then give students a chance to review the comments and questions that were added to their charts and revise their claims if they'd like. Alternatively, you could assign the revisions as a writing homework assignment to be handed in or posted as part of an online discussion.

7. Facilitate a class discussion. How were the explanations alike? Different? Were multiple explanations possible? Then go over one possible explanation together to discuss how the parts of an explanation fit together.

8. Have students individually reflect on the process of constructing explanations: what they learned, what was hard, what they could do to make it easier, and any questions they have. Ask them to turn and talk; then facilitate a group discussion.

Lesson 3: Identifying the Parts of Explanations

Focus Question: What do the parts of a scientific explanation look like in science articles?

Big Idea: Scientists make claims based on evidence (not personal opinion) to answer questions. They use reasoning (big science ideas) to connect the claims and evidence.

Learning Goal: Students will identify the parts of an explanation in a science article.

Materials:

- Copies of a model explanatory article (see Appendix B for some good sources); for our example, we used "The Mysterious Migration of Blackpoll Warblers" (see page 82)

Recommended Time: One fifty-minute session

Lesson:

1. Review the parts of an explanation and how they fit together. Ask students to point them out in the examples that you have used so far.

2. Give students a scientific article to read. Ask students to highlight or underline each part of the explanation and mark it with a Q (question), C (claim), E (evidence), or R (reasoning).

3. After students are finished, ask them to turn and talk with a partner to share their results. Facilitate a whole-class discussion. Do they think that this is a strong explanation? Why? Why not?

PUTTING LESSON 3 INTO ACTION: MIGRATION MYSTERY

Students can read the following article about the migration of blackpoll warblers, which draws from DeLuca et al. (2015) and Johnson (2015), and identify the parts of the explanation.

The Mysterious Migration of Blackpoll Warblers

Many birds that migrate southward during the winter fly along the eastern coast of the United States, stopping along the way to find food. However, ornithologists, scientists who study birds, noticed that tiny blackpoll warblers (songbirds that live in the forests of New England and eastern Canada) were not present along the southern part of the East Coast when the scientists captured and observed birds migrating southward. The scientists also observed blackpoll warblers along the coast of Maine in the fall with large amounts of body fat, indicating that they were preparing for a long flight. In addition, ships in the open ocean reported blackpoll warblers falling from the sky after storms.

As a result, a group of ornithologists wondered if the blackpolls might be flying over the ocean instead of along the coast. To find out the answer to this question, researchers from the University of Massachusetts Amherst put tiny geolocators on thirty-seven blackpolls in Nova Scotia and Vermont and tracked their journey. Five birds were recaptured the following summer near the original Nova Scotia and Vermont capture locations. The data from the geolocators indicated that the birds started flying south in the autumn along the coast of New England and then headed out across the open ocean to the Caribbean in one nonstop, two- to three-day flight (up to 1,721 miles). [See Figure 6.11.] Their ultimate destination was northern South America (northern Colombia or Venezuela). This represents one of the longest nonstop overwater flights for migratory songbirds.

Tagged Blackpoll Warbler	Autumn Migration Data
Warbler A	Left western Nova Scotia (Oct. 14) Stopover in Hispaniola (Oct. 16–17) Arrived northern South America (Oct. 18)
Warbler B	Left western Nova Scotia (Oct. 1) Stopover in Hispaniola (approx. Oct. 3–23) Arrived northern South America (Oct. 24)
Warbler C	Left western Nova Scotia (Sept. 25) Stopover in Puerto Rico (Sept. 27–Oct. 6) Arrived northern South America (Oct. 8)
Warbler D	Left western Long Island/New Jersey (Oct. 21) Stopover in Hispaniola (Oct. 24–31) Arrived in northern South America (Nov. 1)
Warbler E	Left Cape Hatteras (Nov. 4) Stopover in Turks and Caicos (Nov. 6–14) Arrived northern South America (Nov. 15)

Adapted from DeLuca et al. (2015) and Johnson (2015).

Figure 6.11 Blackpoll warbler migration data summary

Students might identify these explanation elements from the blackpoll warbler summary:

- *Question:* What route do blackpoll warblers take when they migrate south in the fall?
- *Claim:* Blackpoll warblers follow the Atlantic coast down to New England and then fly across the open ocean to the Caribbean.
- *Evidence:* Data gathered from geolocators attached to five birds [shown in Figure 6.11].
- *Reasoning:* The autumn migration geolocator data indicate that several of the tagged warblers flew nonstop over the ocean from Nova Scotia or the East Coast to Hispaniola or Puerto Rico. The data did not show them stopping anywhere in between. From Hispaniola or Puerto Rico, the birds flew on to their winter habitats in northern South America.

Lesson 4: Analyzing Scientific Explanations Throughout History

Focus Question: What explanations have supported major scientific theories across time? What are the parts of those explanations?

Big Idea: Scientists make claims based on evidence to answer questions. They use reasoning to connect the claims and evidence. This process has been occurring throughout history.

Learning Goal: Students will research specific scientific theories throughout history and identify the parts of the explanations.

Materials:

- Books, articles, and websites on scientists, such as the BBC Historic Figures site (www.bbc.co.uk/history/historic_figures/) (see the list of model stories in Appendix B for ideas)
- Copies of the Scientific Explanations Throughout History Worksheet (see Figure 6.12)
- Chart paper and markers

Recommended Time: Two to three fifty-minute sessions

Notes: You may need to go through an example first together, perhaps highlighting the question, claim, evidence, and reasoning in different colors. You could create this example on chart paper and post it so students can refer to it.

Lesson:

1. Give students background on how scientists have constructed explanations throughout history. Share that scientific explanations have changed as new tools, data, and understandings have developed.

2. Ask students to work in small groups to research a specific scientific experiment or theory to uncover the explanation behind it. They can record their ideas on the Scientific Explanations Throughout History Worksheet (see Figure 6.12). Depending on your purpose, you may allow students to choose any experiment or theory or something that is related to the topic they are studying.

3. After students have completed their research, assign them to mixed groups so that each group includes students who have researched different theories. Ask them to share what they learned. What are the parts of the explanations? How are they similar? How are they different? How are these explanations similar to and different from the ones they've been constructing in class?

4. Facilitate a class discussion about these questions. Record the findings of each group on a class chart.

The reasoning part of this exercise is difficult for students. We can, in retrospect, come up with reasoning to match the scientists' experiments. But knowing only what they knew then, how would the scientists have reasoned it out? That is a fascinating—albeit difficult—question to answer!

Lesson 5: What Are the Features of a Strong Explanation?

Focus Question: What makes an explanation strong and convincing?

Big Idea: A strong explanation includes a clear claim (relevant to the question), evidence that is relevant, reliable, and sufficient to support the claim, and strong logical reasoning to link the claim and evidence.

Learning Goal: Students will identify the features of a strong explanation.

Materials:

- Examples of a variety and range of more and less effective explanations, such as examples from a previous year's class or ones you create for the lesson
- Chart paper and markers

Recommended Time: One to two fifty-minute classes

Lesson:

1. Ask students to write an answer to the following prompt: What do you think makes an explanation really convincing? Then have them turn and talk with a partner to share their ideas. Hold a class discussion to find out what students are thinking and what you may need to reinforce or review.

Name: _____

Scientific Explanations Throughout History

Your group will research a scientific theory to find out the explanation behind it and identify the parts of the explanation: the question, claim, evidence, and reasoning.

Focus Questions:

- What are the explanations that supported scientific theories throughout history?
- How have scientific theories changed over time?

Scientific Theory:

Scientist(s) Involved in Creating the Theory:

The Explanation Behind the Theory:

  Question:

  Claim:

  Evidence:

  Reasoning:

What did scientists think about this topic before this theory was accepted? How did our thinking change?

Figure 6.12 Scientific Explanations Throughout History Worksheet (reproducible found at www.heinemann.com /products/E08677.aspx)

2. Explain that the class is going to explore what makes an explanation strong and convincing. Begin by having students work in pairs to analyze several explanations, some that are strong and some that could be improved. Ask them to identify which explanations they think are strong and why and to jot down ideas on what makes an explanation strong. (*Note:* You may want to start by providing students only with examples of strong explanations and ask them to share their ideas on what features make the explanations strong.)

3. Ask each pair to turn and talk with another pair to share ideas (and add to their lists, if appropriate). Create a group chart of their ideas. Explain that these are the criteria they will be using when constructing their own explanations. If students do not include key criteria (such as the amount or quality of evidence, for example), ask probing questions to try to guide them.

4. Tell the students that they will be using their class list to create a rubric that they will use to self-assess and peer-assess their explanations. (You might decide to use it for grading as well.) Have the class develop headings and expectations for each level of the rubric. Ask students to work in groups of two to three to create criteria and examples for a specific rubric heading (claim, evidence, or reasoning). When they're ready, have the groups with the same rubric headings confer and come to consensus on what the rubric and examples should look like. Then have the groups share with the entire class to compile the rubric. A sample rubric is shown in Figure 6.13.

5. Now that students have a clear picture of what makes a strong explanation, ask them individually to look again at the less strong explanations. How could they revise these pieces to make them more effective? Each student should rewrite one explanation. (This process will provide evidence of their learning and show you where more examples or instruction may be necessary.)

6. Give students a chance to share their before and after explanations with each other in small groups or pairs and explain why the original explanation was not strong and what they did to strengthen it. You might even have them do a gallery walk or share their revised explanations on a blog, asking them to comment on each other's work. Facilitate a class discussion focusing on the different ways explanations can be strengthened.

Constructing Explanations			
Criterion	**Novice**	**Developing**	**Proficient**
Claim *(An evidence-based statement or conclusion that answers the original question or problem)* A clear, arguable claim is made to answer a question.	Does not make a claim or the claim is not relevant to the question.	Makes an incomplete or unclear claim that is relevant to the question.	Makes a clear, understandable claim relevant to the question.
Evidence *(Scientific data that support the claim)* Relevant and sufficient evidence is provided from accurate, reliable sources to support the claim.	• Does not provide evidence to support the claim or only provides evidence that is not relevant. • The evidence is unreliable.	• Provides relevant but insufficient evidence to support the claim. • Some of the evidence is from accurate, reliable sources.	• Provides relevant and sufficient evidence to support the claim. • All of the evidence is from accurate, reliable sources.
Reasoning *(the big scientific idea or principle that connects the claim and evidence)* Logical reasoning is provided to link the claim and the evidence.	Does not provide logical reasoning to connect the claim and evidence, or provides inappropriate reasoning.	Provides weak reasoning to link the claim and evidence.	Provides strong, logical reasoning to link the claim and evidence.

Figure 6.13 Example rubric for constructing scientific explanations

Lesson 6: Crafting Explanations Based on Our Own Investigation Data

Focus Question: How can we craft explanations based on our own investigation data?

Big Idea: A strong explanation includes a clear claim (relevant to the question), evidence that is relevant, reliable, and sufficient to support the claim, and strong logical reasoning to link the claim and evidence.

Learning Goal: Students will apply what they have learned by crafting explanations based on their own investigation data.

Materials:

- Blank "Observations, Inferences, Claims, and Reasoning" charts
- "Constructing Explanations" rubric (see example in Figure 6.13)
- Chart paper and markers
- Sticky notes

Recommended Time: Two to three fifty-minute classes

Lesson:

1. After students have collected data from a hands-on investigation, explain that they will now have a chance to construct explanations based on their own data. Tell them that they will use an "Observations, Inferences, Claims, and Reasoning" chart to map out their explanations. (*Note:* The first time that your students do this, it may be helpful to have them work in groups or pairs.)

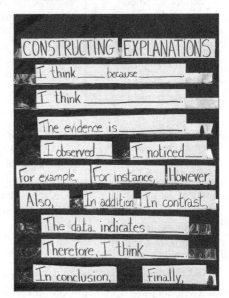

Figure 6.14 When students begin to construct explanations, sentence frames can provide helpful hints on wording and ways to structure their own work.

2. Ask students to make close observations about their data. What do they notice? What new questions do they have? Have them record their ideas on the "Observations, Inferences, Claims, and Reasoning" chart.

3. Now what inferences can they make about their observations? What patterns do they see? What do they think they mean (using their judgment and background knowledge)? What do they think they know that helps them make sense of the observations? Ask them to add their inferences to their charts.

4. Based on their observations and inferences, what claims can they make to answer the question? Which observations are evidence to support the claims?

5. When the students have solidified their explanations, ask them to create visual presentations. Do a gallery walk, giving students sticky notes so they can add comments and questions. Facilitate a class discussion about how their explanations are similar and different.

6. Ask students to write their explanations individually, referring to the class rubric you developed together in the previous lesson and the feedback they received during the gallery walk. At this stage, it is very beneficial to share exemplars of student explanations with the class, going over the parts of the explanation and how they are put together. These exemplars will provide a guide for students. You can also offer necessary support through anchor charts, word walls, and sentence frames such as those in Figure 6.14.

PUTTING LESSON 6 INTO ACTION IN MARK'S CLASSROOM: CREATING MUD STORIES TO PREDICT PAST CLIMATES

As part of our unit on climate, I have students explore the question, What does past climate tell us about the present and future climate? Answering this question involves the study of *proxy data*—indirect measurements such as counts of diatoms (specific microorganisms) and sediment cores. My students analyze actual diatom and sediment core data from different sources. Then they choose one of the locations and write an explanation story based on the data.

The following student work comes from a student's analysis of data from Lake El'gygytgyn, a lake created by an asteroid impact that contains 3.6 million years of continuous sediment depositions.

Climate Change at Lake El'gygytgyn

Claim: Based on the data, I think the sediment core represents an interglacial period that occurred between two Ice Ages during the Pleistocene Epoch.

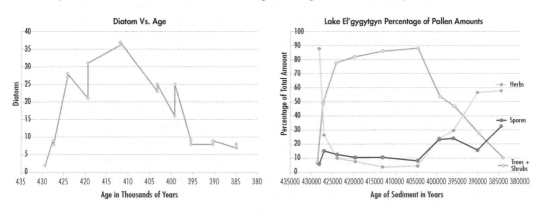

Figures 6.15a–b Lake El'gygytgyn core evidence

Evidence: Our graphs and core description [see Figures 6.15a–b] ultimately support that there was an interglacial period that lasted from about 425,000 to 400,000 years ago because the proxy data corroborates, or matches up. For example, the number of diatoms and the percentage of tree and shrub pollen follow the same pattern. In other words, as the number of diatoms increase or decrease, the percentage of tree and shrub pollen increases or decreases as well. Based on the two graphs, the number of diatoms and percentage of tree and shrub pollen increased 425,000 years ago and remained at that level until 400,000 years ago, when the numbers and percentages dropped. They continue at this low level until the top of the core. Similarly, the data before 425,000 years ago also corroborates because the diatom level and percentage of tree pollen are both very low. Furthermore, based on the core description, it is evident that there is a section in the middle of the core where the sediment is very smooth and does not have any lines or varves. Overall, all three sources for evidence—the core description, diatom graph, and pollen percentage graph—correlate, which means that a clear connection or story can be made between the sediment core and climate change.

Reasoning: Based on the proxy data and its corroboration, I think the sediment core represents an interglacial period that occurred between two Ice Ages during the Pleistocene Epoch. When the number of diatoms and the percentage of tree and shrub pollen increased, it means that it was easier for the organisms to grow during that period of time. Diatoms, trees, and shrubs all need the proper conditions to grow. During a glacial period, the climate would be extremely cold, which would freeze the lake. Therefore, the diatoms would not be able to absorb any sunlight to photosynthesize, as they have been blocked by the ice. This would cause the level of diatoms to drop significantly. However, when the glacial period came to an end and the interglacial period began, the ice would melt and the diatoms could begin to photosynthesize and reproduce once again. Furthermore, it would be harder for trees and shrubs to grow during an ice age because since they are much taller than herbs, the temperature would be lower at a higher altitude, making it harder for the trees to survive. Herbs and spores are much smaller than trees and shrubs, so it would be easier for them to survive extremely cold climates, which is why the percentages of herb and spore pollen decrease as the percentage of tree pollen increases. The percentages of herb and spore pollen also increase as the percentage of tree pollen decreases. Although it seems as though there were not many herbs or spores during the interglacial period, the graph simply shows the percentages of the different types of pollen—not the total amount. This means that there could have been a large amount of herb and spore pollen during the interglacial period, but the amount of tree pollen was just higher, and therefore had a higher percentage. The number of diatoms and percentages of different types of pollen, examples of proxy data, are extremely helpful for determining past climate because they come directly from living things. Unlike the core description, these climate proxies help us visualize the data more clearly, which helps us recognize patterns more easily. When climate proxies corroborate, it means that a valid claim can be made about the relationship between sediment and climate change.

This student made a very clear connection between the evidence and her claim, and her reasoning is sound. She demonstrated clearly how a cold climate could influence the ability of plants to grow and how the diatom population would drop when the lake froze over.

Lesson 7: Matching Our Explanations to the Purpose and Audience

Focus Question: How can we take our original explanations and transform them into stories that effectively communicate the big ideas to the appropriate audience in an engaging way?

Big Ideas: Engaging and interesting explanation stories clearly communicate the key elements (question, claim, evidence, and reasoning) to the target audience in a way that is concise and interesting. They include many of the elements of effective science stories.

Learning Goal: Students will turn their original explanations into polished pieces by including the elements of good science stories that are appropriate for the purpose and audience. To do this, they will look at many examples of explanation stories.

Materials:

- Model explanation stories (see Appendix B for suggestions)
- Chart paper and markers

Recommended Time: Two to three fifty-minute sessions

Notes: This lesson should be used after your students have mastered the basic practice of constructing explanations so they can focus on tailoring their explanations to their purpose and audience.

Lesson:

1. In small groups, give students two explanations to analyze: a basic explanation and an explanation that includes elements of effective science stories. (At this point, don't tell students the difference between the samples.) Have them consider these questions:

   - How are the two explanations the same? How are they different?
   - Which one do you think someone would rather read, listen to, or watch? Why?
   - What is the purpose of each explanation?
   - Who is the audience?

   We suggest giving each group different stories to look at in order to foster richer conversations about the features of engaging explanations.

2. Mix up the groups. Ask students to share their ideas and come to consensus on which explanations they find more engaging, and make a class list of their ideas. (Guide students toward including the elements of effective science stories, listed in Figure 2.2. However, students may have new ideas to add to the list, which is great!) Explain that they will be using this list to incorporate the elements of effective science stories into their explanations.

3. Have them share their thoughts on the purposes and audiences of the stories they examined. How might an explanation crafted for presentation at a scientific conference be different from an explanatory story that will be published online or in a newspaper?

4. Give students (individually or in pairs) the chance to analyze additional model stories. Have students highlight and label the elements of effective science stories that they find and think about what the purpose and audience might be.

5. With the whole group, model the process of transforming an explanation for a general audience. Post the before and after explanations so students can clearly see what was done. Brainstorm a class list of ways to improve explanation stories that will be shared with the general public, other students, or younger children (see Figure 6.16).

6. Let students choose one of the explanations they have created to fine-tune based on what they have just learned about the elements of effective science stories. At first, you may want to allow them to work in pairs. Another option is to work on one or two elements at a time, so students aren't overwhelmed.

7. Be sure to allow lots of time for peer review, giving students multiple opportunities to learn from each other and share ideas.

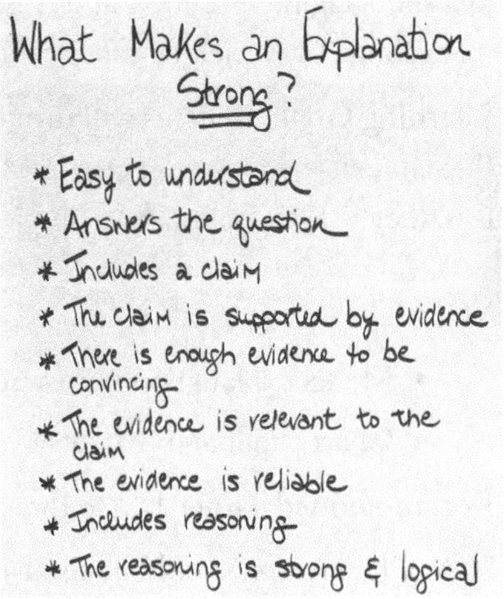

What Makes an Explanation Strong?

* Easy to understand
* Answers the question
* Includes a claim
* The claim is supported by evidence
* There is enough evidence to be convincing
* The evidence is relevant to the claim
* The evidence is reliable
* Includes reasoning
* The reasoning is strong & logical

Figure 6.16 Creating and posting a class chart of ways to make explanation stories engaging for general audiences can help students remember ways to improve their explanations.

Lesson 8: Setting the Stage for Critiquing Explanations

Focus Question: How do scientists critique and review the explanations of others in order to strengthen their explanations and determine which explanation is best?

Big Idea: Scientists critique and review the explanations of others in order to help strengthen their explanations and work collaboratively to find the strongest explanation to answer a question. In this way, they collectively build understanding about our world.

Learning Goal: Students will apply what they learned in the previous lessons about analyzing and revising explanations to their own work. They will begin to practice critiquing each other's explanations in order to help strengthen their explanations.

Materials:

- "Constructing Explanations" rubric that your class created earlier (see Lesson 5)
- Chart paper and markers

Recommended Time: One to two fifty-minute classes

Lesson:

1. Review the idea that scientists are always seeking to strengthen their explanations and find the best explanation to answer a specific question. Ask students, "If several scientists come up with different explanations to answer a question, how can we determine which one is the strongest?" Then ask the class, "What happens when the scientists are located all over the world? How do they find the strongest explanation? How do they help each other strengthen their explanations?"

2. Building on ideas shared by students, explain the different ways that scientists refine and critique each other's work (conferences, online blogs, informal discussions, and publishing in scientific journals). Tell the class that they will be participating in this process of refining and critiquing, but first they need to help develop norms for this process.

3. Ask students what norms or rules they think are necessary in order to give and receive quality feedback on explanations.

   - Create a class chart or Y-chart (see Figure 6.17 for an example).
   - Have students identify *observable* features. Ask students to identify what good critiquing behavior looks, sounds, or feels like. (Rather than "Be nice," for example, they might say, "Sounds like respectful language." This could

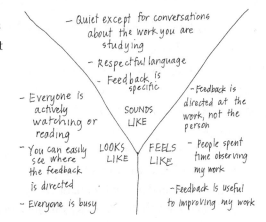

Figure 6.17 Example Y-chart recording norms for critiquing the explanations of others

lead to a fruitful conversation about what respectful language is—no put-downs, disagreeing respectfully, and so on). Also encourage students to be specific in their feedback.

4. Give students an explanation to critique (not one from their current class) using the "Constructing Explanations" rubric. Ask them to focus on what makes the explanation

strong and how it could be improved. In small groups, assign one student to take the role of the explanation author as the others provide feedback. Alternatively, you could facilitate a whole-class discussion, providing feedback to a virtual author. During this process, challenge them to be very specific (e.g., "I like the way you visually presented your evidence to support your claim. It's very clear and easy to understand.").

5. Next, ask students to critique each other's explanations with partners, in small groups, in whole-class discussions, via gallery walks, or via blogs. Throughout these critiquing sessions, refer students back to the norms if needed and ask if any norms need to be changed or added. Encourage them to connect to the ideas of others and use direct quotes from the explanations to make their points.

6. Periodically have students reflect on what types of feedback helped them and what types did not. It may be helpful to keep a running list (on chart paper, for example) that you can have students refer to in subsequent feedback sessions.

7. Give students multiple and varied opportunities to critique explanations so that it becomes a natural part of their learning.

Putting Lesson 8 into Action in Mark's Classroom: Critiquing During a Science Talk

The students in my class had been exploring crystal growth. To start a science talk on this topic, the entire class sat together in a circle. We reviewed the class norms for science talks and discussed the fact that part of our purpose in this talk was to challenge each other's ideas. Then I posed the question, "What do you think are the best conditions for growing the biggest crystals?" The discussion flowed freely, with participation from most students.

Students asked each other to explain themselves better. Some shared graphs as a way of defending their claims. One student challenged another's explanation of why her experiment turned out the way it did. Another student asked the group to think about the basic ideas behind crystal growth, because he was confused about this process and how it connected to his experiment. Two students tried to describe their mental models of how crystals grow and why some grow larger than others. Students didn't raise their hands, and yet the tone of the discussion remained respectful and mature:

"My data shows me that when we cool the crystals more slowly, they come out bigger."

"I don't understand why you think cooling rate matters. Can you explain your idea again?"

"How many times did you do this experiment? Is it possible that this only happened one time?"

"Why do you think the rate of cooling makes a difference?"

"Wait. I'm confused. How is it that crystals are forming anyway?"

My students were not just learning on their own or in small groups; they were part of an authentic, self-driven scientific learning community.

How Do We Weave Explanatory Stories into Our Teaching?

When we look for places to bring student science stories into our curriculum, we always ask ourselves, *What is our purpose for having students create their own science stories? How do the stories support the learning goals for the science content or science practices?* Our goals for explanation stories may center on having students deepen their thinking; craft explanations and be able to critique the explanations of others; demonstrate their understanding; or communicate their ideas in writing or orally.

Tips on planning for student explanation stories are provided in Figure 6.18.

Questions to Ask When Planning	Suggestions
• What activities will students be doing? What materials will they be using? • What types of evidence will students be gathering? • When are crucial points for them to craft explanations based on their observations? • What scaffolding and modeling will I do to help them craft their explanations? • When will asking students to critique and receive feedback on explanation stories help them deepen their thinking and improve their explanations?	• When choosing when to have students craft explanatory stories, make sure they have had a chance to collect many pieces of evidence to support their claims. • Facilitate a science talk before students write their explanations so they can rehearse and fine-tune their thinking. • Ask students to write their explanatory stories on the class blog and give feedback to two or three peers (this works well before a science talk).

Figure 6.18 Tips for integrating explanatory stories into your curriculum

7 Informational Stories of Science

The important thing in science is not so much to obtain new facts as to discover new ways of thinking about them.

—Sir William Lawrence Bragg

A Story from Janet

Sunday nights were special in my house when I was growing up. At 7:30, we would gather around the big console TV (which got three channels—or four, when the weather was just right) and watch *The Wonderful World of Disney*. This was a family variety-type program hosted by Walt Disney that featured nature documentaries, cartoons, and live-action stories. During this hour, we got a glimpse into places and people far outside our realm in rural Pennsylvania.

With Walt at the helm on those Sunday evenings, I raced with cheetahs on the African savanna, hunted with snow leopards in Nepal, struggled to survive in the heat of the Sonoran Desert, and frolicked in the geysers of Yellowstone with black bears—all from the comfy blue couch in my living room. The incredible visuals and playful narratives of Walt's stories brought these exotic lands and creatures into my world in a way that books could not. Afterward, I would break out our trusty, well-worn *World Book* (and go to the library) to learn more. (This was long before the age of the Internet.) What other animals lived in the wondrous world of Yellowstone? What did they eat in the winter? What forces caused those amazing geysers? I was full of questions.

As Janet did in her quest for knowledge after watching *The Wonderful World of Disney*, scientists often gather and synthesize information from other sources in order to answer questions. Our purpose may be to learn about something that we cannot investigate or to find out what other scientists have discovered about a topic prior to doing an investigation ourselves. Every time we consult a field guide, do an Internet search on a topic, or search for scientific news briefs, articles, or books, we are consulting our scientific colleagues at large and are thinking critically about what information we can rely on.

Informational Stories: Synthesizing Information Gathered from Others

Informational stories share information that has been synthesized from other sources (not one's own investigations). The purpose of these stories may be to share a sense of wonder, teach others, persuade others, or look at existing findings in a new way. Or perhaps students have additional questions after they conduct their own hands-on inquiry investigations that they can't answer on their own. Like explanatory stories, informational stories include the features of effective stories and must be crafted in a way that targets the purpose, audience, and setting. However, explanations depend on firsthand inquiry or analyzing the data of others to construct an explanation, while informational stories require students to do in-depth research to find nuggets from other sources that they can use to teach their audience about a topic.

Crafting Informational Stories

A lot has to happen behind the scenes to end up with a powerful informational story. Figure 7.1 summarizes the steps, which we explore in more detail here.

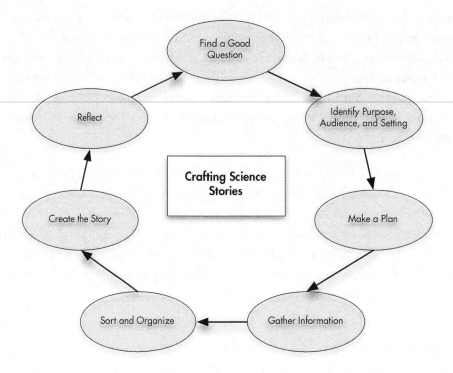

Figure 7.1 Crafting Science Stories Visual (reproducible found at www.heinemann.com/products/E08677.aspx)

1. Find a good question.
   - Brainstorm questions that might be explored by thinking individually, talking with others, and browsing sources
   - Select a question that you're really curious about.

2. Identify the purpose, audience, and setting.
   - Choose a clear purpose for the story.
   - Know who the audience will be and where and how you will need to present the story (online, in person, etc.).

3. Make a plan.
   - Define what information is needed to answer the question.
   - Map out possible options for finding pertinent and reliable info (experts, Internet search engines, books, articles, etc.).
   - Identify important keywords to use for searching.

4. Gather information.

- Gather information that is relevant and useful (always keeping the question in mind).

- Search logically and strategically using targeted searches and search engines.

- Use strategies to manage information and share it with others (such as social bookmarking tools).

- Evaluate sources (and the information they provide) to ensure that the information you're gathering is reliable.

5. Sort and organize.

- Sort and organize the information you've gathered.

- Create an outline or storyboard for your informational story.

- Determine if more information is needed and gather it if necessary.

6. Craft the informational story and share it with others.

- Compile the information to answer the question in an informational story, using the elements of effective science stories (see Chapter 2) while focusing on your purpose, audience, and setting (see Chapter 5).

- Attribute all sources appropriately.

- Share the story with others (including creatively sharing information with others worldwide via the Internet and social networking tools).

7. Reflect on the experience.

- Reflect on what you learned, how you learned it, and what additional questions you have.

In the following sections, we take a deep dive into the process of crafting informational stories. If this process is new to your students, we recommend modeling the steps, doing examples together, and showing many exemplars along the way.

Finding a Good Question

Just like explanatory stories, informational stories begin with curiosity and questions. The framing of the question is critical. We've all seen cookie-cutter planet reports and ecosystem reports—often with the same format and headings. In many cases, students are assigned a topic without any type of focus question (certainly not one that the students have any interest in). Not only are these boring to read, but they are boring to create as well.

Instead of asking students to write about the structure of Earth, for example, brainstorm related questions with them and let them each choose an intriguing one to explore and craft a story about. Some questions that might come up: What would it look like if we drilled down into the center of Earth? How do we know what the inside of Earth is made of? Is it really like the movie *Journey to the Center of the Earth*? Why or why not?

Good questions for informational stories are deep and intriguing and entice us to look at something in a new way. Most of all, they draw people in so that they want to delve into the subject to learn more, synthesize the information, and then pull it all together to answer the question. It's much more than simply rehashing an encyclopedia entry! Here are some more example questions:

- Why do some animals have brains and others don't?
- Why are stem cells so important to biology, and why are they so controversial?
- What is it like in the deepest part of the ocean? Why is it like that?
- How do we know what we know about distant objects in the universe, just by observing these objects from Earth?
- What are the most efficient ways to generate electricity?
- Why do some chemical reactions occur faster than others?

Generating Questions: The Question Formulation Technique

The Question Formulation Technique is a great strategy for teaching students to generate their own questions (for all types of stories). This method, created by the Right Question Institute (see http://rightquestion.org/education/#wrap), provides a logical sequence for helping students find and fine-tune questions:

1. *Provide a question focus:* Give students a focus (a statement, a visual, an interesting object, etc.) to spark questions around a particular topic and engage their interest.

2. *Share rules for producing questions:*
   - Ask as many questions as you can.
   - Do not stop to discuss, judge, or answer the questions.
   - Write down every question exactly as it is stated.
   - Change any statement into a question.

3. *Produce questions:* Invite students to freely brainstorm all kinds of questions related to the question focus (while following the rules). This is a chance for them to unleash their inner curiosity with absolutely no judgment! Some of the initial questions created in response to our colleague Maxine Hunter's question focus, "Birds have brains; jellyfish don't," are shown in Figure 7.2.

4. *Categorize and improve questions:* Discuss the difference between open-ended and closed-ended questions. (An open-ended question is a question that requires a lot of

thought and leads to a full, detailed answer, whereas a closed-ended question is one that can be answered with yes or no or a one- or two-word answer). After generating their own definitions, have students sort their questions into open- and closed-ended questions. Ask them to share their ideas about when each type of question is helpful and then practice changing some of their closed-ended questions to open-ended ones. For instance, the closed-ended question, Do beavers hibernate in the winter? might change to, How do beavers survive in the harsh cold of winter?

Here are some examples of student-improved questions for "Birds have brains; jellyfish don't":

BIRDS HAVE BRAINS, JELLYFISH DON'T

WHY DON'T JELLYFISH HAVE BRAINS?
DO ALL BIRDS HAVE SAME SIZE BRAIN?
HOW DO JELLYFISH MOVE WITHOUT A BRAIN?
*WHAT CONTROLS THEIR BODY SYSTEMS?
WHAT DO BIRDS' BRAINS DO?
ARE JELLYFISH MORE PRIMATIVE THAN BIRDS?
DO BIRD BRAINS LOOK LIKE HUMAN BRAINS?
*WHAT'S DIFFERENT ABOUT BIRDS & JELLYFISH?
DO OTHER SEA CREATURES HAVE/LACK BRAINS?
WHAT OTHER ANIMALS DON'T HAVE BRAINS?
*WHAT IS THE BASIC CRITERIA TO BE CONSIDERED A BRAIN?
HOW DO JELLYFISH 'KNOW' WHAT TO DO?

Figure 7.2 Initial questions generated by sixth graders in Maxine Hunter's class

- How can jellyfish live without a brain? Is their whole body a brain?
- How did birds and jellyfish evolve?
- How are jellyfish, birds, and humans similar? Different?
- How are invertebrates and vertebrates similar? Different?
- What are the advantages of having a brain? The disadvantages?
- When did brains appear in evolutionary history? Do scientists have ideas about why brains appeared?

5. *Determine next steps*: Ask students to share one or two questions that they really want to explore. Students may then choose one question that they all pursue, groups may choose different questions, or individual students may select the question of their choice.

6. *Reflect*: Ask students to reflect on what they did and why they did it. Ask, "How did this process help you generate, fine-tune, and use questions? Next time, how could we improve it?"

Considering Purpose, Audience, and Setting and Making a Plan

After students identify their questions, they need to think about the story's purpose, audience, and setting, as we discussed in detail in Chapter 5. Then students will plan what information they need to gather and how they will gather it before they start their research. Doing this up front lets students target the best information sources.

Possible questions to ask students in this stage include the following:

- What information do you think you'll need to find to answer the question?
- Who are the experts in the field? What organizations are they affiliated with?
- What keywords will help you find information? (Be as specific as you can.)

Gathering Information

Now comes the fun part! Students begin searching for the puzzle pieces of information that will all eventually come together to answer their question. Conducting research can be challenging for students. Sometimes, they will need to gather general information about the topic before digging more deeply. Students can feel overwhelmed when they uncover too many resources or too much information about a topic or frustrated when they cannot find enough information. Throughout this messy process, we try to empower students to troubleshoot on their own and to help each other out rather than give them all the answers.

We encourage students to use a mix of books, online databases that might be available in the school library, and the Internet. However, the Internet is the research tool of the future, so we must prepare students to use it effectively. Searching online brings to the surface a whole slew of novel questions and issues that we need to address.

Searching the Internet Strategically

Students have a virtual global library at their fingertips. We must teach them how to search strategically so they can get what they need as easily and quickly as possible. However, these strategies are effective only if students have a handle on exactly what they're looking for. This is why it's so important to have a good question and a plan before they even come close to hitting the Internet.

A starting point for students is learning what a site's address can tell us about the source of the information. Is the information from a government agency (.gov), an educational institution (.edu or .ac), a K–12 school (.k12 or .sch), a business (.com), or some other kind of organization (.org, .net, and so on)? What does that tell us about how reliable the source is? In general, government and academic sites are more likely to have reliable information. Anyone can buy the .com, .net, and .org extensions.

With a basic knowledge of web addresses and their research plan, students can use the sophisticated capabilities of search engines to zoom in on the information they need. Some helpful Google search operators are shown in Figure 7.3.

Search Operator	Purpose of the Search Operator	Topic of Search	Example Search
" "	Find pages that have the exact words designated in quotes	The *New Horizons* spacecraft that flew by Pluto in July 2015	"New Horizons spacecraft"
- (must be preceded by a space)	Exclude a term from a search	Pluto (the dwarf planet), not Pluto (the Disney cartoon dog)	Pluto -dog
OR	Find pages that include either of two terms	Pluto and/or *New Horizons* spacecraft	Pluto OR "New Horizons spacecraft"
*	Wildcard	Edwin Hubble (including entries for Edwin Powell Hubble and Edwin P. Hubble)	"Edwin * Hubble"
…	Search for a range of numbers	Discoveries related to Pluto from 1930 to 1980	"Pluto discoveries" 1930…1980
filetype:	Find certain types of files that end in a specific suffix (pdf, ppt, mp3, mp4, doc, jpg, xls, swf, etc.)	Flash files about the *New Horizons* Pluto flyby	Pluto flyby filetype: swf
allintext: or allintitle:	Search for multiple words in the text or title of web pages	The geology of Pluto's mountains	allintext: Pluto geology mountains
location:	Search for web pages from specific locations	Astronomy observatories in the United States	astronomy observatories location: United States
site:	Restrict search to the site or domain you specify	Information on Pluto from U.S. government websites	Pluto site:gov

continues

Search Operator	Purpose of the Search Operator	Topic of Search	Example Search
source:	Restrict search to articles from specific news sources	Find news articles about Pluto from reliable news sources	Pluto source:New York Times Pluto source:BBC

Adapted from Google Guide, by Nancy Blachman (www.googleguide.com), and "Google Search Tips: Google Operators," by MIT Libraries (http://libguides.mit.edu/c.php?g=176061&p=1159512).

Figure 7.3 Google Search Operators Chart (reproducible found at www.heinemann.com/products /E08677.aspx)

JUDGING THE RELIABILITY OF THE INFORMATION

Since anyone with access to a computer and the Internet can post information, it's critical that we teach students how to be savvy consumers of the information they gather. For this purpose, we like to use the Information Reliability Test, which was renamed and adapted from the CRAAP test, originally compiled by the Meriam Library (2010). With this test, students use five criteria to evaluate the reliability of websites (and any other information source). (See Figure 7.4.)

Reliability Criterion	Questions to Ask
Current: Is the information up-to-date?	• When was the information published or posted? • Has the information been revised or updated? • Are the links functional? • Does your topic require current information, or will older sources work as well?
Relevant: Does the information answer your focus research question?	• Does the information relate to your topic or answer your question? • Who is the intended audience? • Is it a primary or secondary source? • Is the information at the appropriate level (i.e., not too elementary or advanced for your needs)? • Have you looked at a variety of sources before determining this is one you will use? • Would you be comfortable citing this source?

Reliability Criterion	Questions to Ask
Credible: Is the source of the information reputable and reliable?	• Who is the author, publisher, source, or sponsor? • Is the author identified by name? • What are the author's credentials and organizational affiliations? • Can you uncover any information about the author if you do a search? • Can you find this author cited by other sources? • Is the author qualified to write on this topic? • Can the author be contacted via email or phone if you have questions? • Does the URL reveal anything about the author or source?
Accurate: Is the content reliable, honest, and correct?	• Where does the information come from? • Is the information supported by evidence (and does it cite original sources)? • Has the information been reviewed or refereed? • Can you verify any of the information in another source or from personal knowledge? • Are there facts or ideas you know to be false or in conflict with other information you found in your research? • Does the language or tone seem unbiased and free of emotion? • Are there spelling, grammar, or typographical errors? • Is the site free of advertising?
Perspective: What is the point of view or purpose of the information? Is it presented objectively?	• What is the purpose of the information? Is it to inform, teach, sell, entertain, or persuade? • Do the authors or sponsors make their intentions or purpose clear? • Is the information fact, opinion, or propaganda? • Does the point of view appear objective and impartial? • Are there political, ideological, cultural, religious, institutional, or personal biases? • Are alternate points of view represented?

Adapted from the CRAAP Test, developed by the Meriam Library at California State University, Chico (www.csuchico.edu/lins /handouts/eval_websites.pdf).

Figure 7.4 Information Reliability Test (reproducible found at www.heinemann.com/products/E08677.aspx)

Sorting and Organizing Information

There are many ways for students to sort and organize their notes: lay all their notecards out and categorize them, sort their information in a Word file, or go visual by creating a big colorful chart to summarize the information. Then they can start with the question they're trying to answer and map out the logical sequence of the story. What information do they actually need? (Some extraneous but cool info may need to be jettisoned.) What information is missing? They can share their outlines with each other for additional feedback.

Lessons for Teaching Students to Craft Informational Science Stories

Informational stories sometimes get bogged down in technical vocabulary and dry facts, stifling any excitement or sense of curiosity. In this section, we share five lessons that you can use to teach your students how to communicate science stories effectively, letting their creativity and passion take center stage:

- Lesson 1: Introducing and Analyzing Informational Stories
- Lesson 2: Transforming Informational Stories
- Lesson 3: Setting the Stage for Our Own Informational Stories
- Lesson 4: Gathering Information for Informational Stories
- Lesson 5: Crafting Our Own Informational Stories

Lesson 1: Introducing and Analyzing Informational Stories

Focus Questions: What are informational stories? What elements make informational stories effective?

Big Idea: Engaging and interesting informational stories clearly communicate the key elements to the target audience in a way that is concise and interesting.

Learning Goals: Students will identify what informational stories are and identify the elements that make them good.

Materials:

- A variety of model informational stories in many forms (see Appendix B for some suggestions)
- Chart paper and markers

Recommended Time: Two or three fifty-minute sessions

Notes: If you have already done a similar activity with your students around science explanations (Chapter 6) or personal stories (Chapter 8), it might be interesting to have students compare the elements of the different kinds of stories. How are they alike? How are they different? Why?

Lesson:

1. Explain that sometimes we need to gather information from other sources to answer our questions and create our own informational science stories. Tell students that they are going to look at different informational stories and identify the elements that make them effective. These stories will be models for the ones they will be creating later.

2. In small groups, ask students to watch, read, or listen to a model informational story. We often find it interesting to give each group a different story type—text, video, podcast, infographic, and so on—so they can see how the elements of good informational stories look in different formats. If possible, include student informational stories in this activity as well as ones gathered from other sources. Have students jot down what elements they notice in the good stories. Encourage them to focus on these questions:

   - What elements of the story help the audience learn the information?
   - What techniques does the author use?
   - What elements of the story help engage the audience? How?
   - What is the intriguing question being answered here?
   - What made the author curious enough to research this topic in the first place?
   - How did the author uncover mystery and intrigue behind this topic, rather than just report the facts?
   - How did the author grab listeners or readers to spark their curiosity and interest?
   - Were personal connections made between the author and the audience? How?
   - How did the author craft the story to be accessible to the audience?

3. After they are finished, have the students share their ideas with the class. As you listen to their thoughts, bring up any of the key elements of science stories that they may not have mentioned (see Figure 2.2 on pages 19–20). It's also possible that students will come up with different, very valid ideas (which is great!), or they might frame the elements differently (also great—any time students can frame ideas in their own words, it's much

more meaningful for them). Create a class list you can come back to later. Explain that students will use this list of criteria when crafting their own informational stories. (You can also use this list to create a class informational story rubric with students; see Chapter 6, page 87, for more on creating rubrics.)

Lesson 2: Transforming Informational Stories

Focus Question: How can we transform informational excerpts into engaging informational stories?

Big Ideas: Engaging and interesting informational stories clearly communicate the key elements to the target audience in a way that is concise and interesting.

Learning Goals: Students will apply what they learned about the key elements of informational stories by improving a dull science information excerpt.

Materials:

- An example of a dry science informational story (video, text, podcast, etc.)
- Chart paper and markers

Recommended Time: One to two fifty-minute sessions

Note: In this activity, we suggest that you give every group the same story to transform.

Lesson:

1. Give student groups the story, and tell them that they will be using what they have learned to share the same information in a more engaging way. Specify an audience for the transformed story (second graders, the general public, etc.). Encourage students to change the form of the information if they'd like (change text into a visual, for example) and to use their creativity and imagination.

2. When students have completed this task, post the students' work and do a gallery walk so the entire class can observe the improved versions from each group. Encourage students to write their questions and comments on sticky notes for each group. Allow time for students to consider the feedback from others and revise their stories if necessary.

3. Facilitate a class discussion: "What techniques did we use to transform the stories? What did we learn from this experience?" Chart student ideas.

Putting Lesson 2 into Action in Mark's Classroom: Transforming a Story About Diffusion

I asked my seventh-grade students to transform a piece about diffusion and breathing for the purpose of educating a fifth-grade audience about how oxygen gets into cells when you breathe. Here's the original:

Diffusion and Breathing

Diffusion happens when particles move from where they are highly concentrated (hypertonic) to where there is a low concentration (hypotonic). It's important to remember that this movement is a consequence of random movements in speed and direction of all molecules or atoms.

The process of diffusion will continue until the concentration is equal (isotonic) throughout the system. Since temperature is proportional to the average speed of the particles, when the temperature increases, the rate of diffusion will increase.

One example of diffusion is how oxygen enters the body during breathing. The lungs expand and bring air into tiny air sacs called alveoli. Alveoli are surrounded by blood in tiny blood vessels called capillaries. This blood is deoxygenated blood that has been pumped by the heart from the body's cells back to the lungs.

The air that comes into the alveoli has a higher concentration of oxygen molecules than what is in the blood cells in the surrounding capillaries. By diffusion, the oxygen molecules move from where it is hypertonic (the alveoli) to where it is hypotonic (the blood cells).

One group created the following transformed story.

Riding with an Oxygen Molecule

Take a deep breath, and imagine if you could go inside your body to see what it does with the oxygen. Imagine you're on an oxygen molecule and you are going down into your lungs. The oxygen goes into your lungs to give [y]our [sic] blood oxygen. After that they go into the blood, which happens by diffusion. Diffusion is when molecules move from an area where there are many molecules to an area where there aren't many molecules. This happens because of random movements! The molecules are going really fast and they bump into other molecules and eventually spread out. It's like if you're in a bumper car, everyone is just bumping into each other. Eventually after bumping around the bumper cars will spread out.

Your oxygen molecule is just getting bumped around randomly so it's hard for you to hold on. The oxygen molecule will keep bumping into other molecules but eventually it will get into your blood. At first the blood had no oxygen in it until oxygen molecules like yours get bumped into the blood.

Diffusion is a very difficult concept for many middle schoolers because it requires students to visualize invisible air molecules and keep in mind assumptions about the random motion of these molecules. In this story, the students were able to explain in simple terms the randomness of diffusion and how it applies to the intake of oxygen in the lungs. The students tried to make the connection clear to a younger audience and, in the process, they were checking their own understanding of these complex ideas. It might have made the story clearer had I asked the students to explore more deeply how the "spreading out" happens, perhaps through a drawing.

Lesson 3: Setting the Stage for Our Own Informational Stories

Focus Questions: How do we create informational stories? What do we need to do before we start gathering information for our informational stories?

Big Idea: Creating an informational science story involves (1) finding a good question; (2) identifying the story's purpose, audience, and setting; (3) making a plan for gathering information; (4) gathering information; (5) sorting and organizing the information; (6) creating the story; and (7) reflecting on the experience.

Learning Goals: Students will learn about the process of crafting informational stories and begin setting the stage for their own informational stories by identifying questions, purpose, audience, and setting and making a plan.

Materials:

- Crafting Science Stories Visual (see Figure 7.1)
- Sticky notes or sentence strips

Recommended Time: Two to three fifty-minute sessions

Note: We suggest having students work in groups of two or three for this lesson, especially if the process of crafting stories is new for them.

Lesson:

Overview of the Steps Involved in Crafting Informational Stories

1. Tell students that they're ready to craft informational stories of their own. Ask them what they think they'll need to do during this process and in what order. Record student ideas.

2. Share the steps involved in crafting informational stories. We find it helpful to post the visual in Figure 7.1 in the classroom. Show how the students' ideas fit into this scheme. Explain that this will be the process they'll use to create their informational stories.

3. Ask students what questions they have about the steps involved in this process. How is it similar to or different from what they have done in the past? What steps do they feel comfortable with? Which ones are more unfamiliar? This will give you an idea of which steps to focus more time and energy on.

Finding a Question

1. Explain that all science stories start with a good question. Use a class brainstorming session or a more formal question-generating strategy to help students individually generate and fine-tune their questions. You may want to give students the main topic for their questions (e.g., ecosystems or plate tectonics) so that they connect to your curriculum, or you can allow them to choose questions on any science topic. (See Chapter 3 for more on finding good questions.)

2. Ask students to share their questions and get feedback from each other.

   - Is the question open-ended (i.e., does it requires more than a yes, no, or one-word answer)?

   - Is it deep and intriguing?

   - Does the question encourage us to look at a topic in a new way?

   - Is it interesting?

3. Post all the questions on sticky notes or sentence strips and have students sort them, putting like questions together. Then they can self-select their groups by choosing a question that they'd like to research. If many students want to pursue the same question, they can break into several groups. This is a great way to show how the same question can be answered in many different ways.

Identifying the Purpose, Audience, and Setting and Making a Plan

1. We suggest brainstorming different possible purposes, audiences, and settings with the class so students know what options are available. (See Chapter 5 for more on making these choices.) Depending on your goals, you may want to choose one purpose, audience, or setting (or all three) for the whole class or allow each group to choose its own. You also need to identify what form(s) the stories can take—will you allow students to choose the form of their story (text, visual, video, infographic, etc.), or will you give them specific choices? This depends a great deal on the level of independence among your students and on who the intended audience is.

2. Ask students: "Why is it important to make a plan before starting to do research for informational stories?" Review the planning process:

   - Define what information is needed to answer the question.

   - Map out possible options for finding pertinent and reliable info.

   - Identify important keywords to use for searching.

3. Share your expectations with students, including the number and types of sources you want them to use or specific types of information you want them to include. (Preparing a rubric or guidelines is really helpful for both you and your students.)

4. Ask each group to dissect their question and think carefully about what information they might need to answer it. You may want to model the process with the whole class using an example. Some students may want to create a list. Others may choose to create a concept map or some other type of visual to record their ideas.

5. Next, students will need to identify possible sources to find the information they need. Ask students where they might go for information (e.g., the Internet, books, online databases in the school library, experts). At this point, they don't need to list specific books, but they will need to think about what the topics of the books and other resources might be. Mention that sometimes, if we don't know much about a topic, we need to read some general information first before choosing more specific sources.

6. If students will be searching the Internet, discuss how they can design their searches effectively. Review the importance of choosing good keywords and search tools (you might share a list of operators like the one in Figure 7.3.) Model some example searches with the class. Then have students identify keywords and searches for their own questions. If students need more support, use the next lesson to provide additional help.

Lesson 4: Gathering Information for Informational Stories

Focus Question: How can we effectively find reliable information on the Internet?

Big Ideas: Scientists need to be selective about choosing what information to include in their stories to make sure it's reliable.

Learning Goals: Students will perform strategic Internet searches and identify reliable sources on the Internet.

Materials:

- Computers with access to the Internet
- Copies of the Google Search Operators Chart (Figure 7.3)

- Copies of the Information Reliability Test (Figure 7.4)
- Copies of the Internet Search Scavenger Hunt (Figure 7.5)

Recommended Time: Two to three fifty-minute sessions

Lesson:

1. Review with students how to use search operators to refine their Internet searches. Distribute copies of Figure 7.3. Demonstrate the use of the operators using the examples on the chart. As you do this, ask students for their ideas on searches that might be fine-tuned using each search operator and try them out in real time.

2. Ask students to individually write a response to these questions: "Should we believe everything we see on the Internet? Why or why not?" Have students turn and talk, and then facilitate a class discussion.

3. Probe further by asking, "How can we tell if information we find on the Internet is true and reliable?" Record student ideas; then ask students to put them into categories. Share the Information Reliability Test (Figure 7.4), adding ideas that students did not mention to your class list. Give each student a copy of the list for future use. If needed, review the information about domains described previously (e.g., that .gov and .edu sites are more likely to contain reliable information).

4. Tell students that you're going to use the criteria together to check out a website or video. Working in pairs, have students go to one of the following pages. (All students should go to the same page.) Ask them to use their criteria to determine if they think the information is reliable. Why or why not?

   - "BBC: Spaghetti-Harvest in Ticino" (www.youtube.com/watch?v=tVo_wkxH9dU)
   - Pacific Northwest Tree Octopus (http://zapatopi.net/treeoctopus/)
   - How to Charge an iPod Using Electrolytes and an Onion (www.youtube.com/watch?v=GfPJeDssBOM)

5. Project the website or video on the board so the entire class can see it and then facilitate a class discussion about what students thought about the reliability of the information. Make sure they use evidence to support their claims. Explain that these sources are extreme examples of unreliable information on the Internet, but they clearly show why we need to be careful in believing everything we encounter on the Internet!

6. Choose another website (a more reliable one) and ask students to analyze it. What do they think and why?

7. Explain that before they do their own Internet searches, they'll get a chance to practice by doing an Internet scavenger hunt. Split the class into teams of two to three and hand out the Internet Search Scavenger Hunt sheets (Figure 7.5).

8. After students have completed the scavenger hunt, come together as a group and talk about their experiences. Which operators worked the best? How did they use them? What did they learn from this activity?

Name: _____

Internet Search Scavenger Hunt

Item You Need to Find	What search will you use?	Results (How did it work? How could you refine your search? How do you know the information is reliable?)
Original source of the quote "Science is a way of thinking much more than it is a body of knowledge."		
Information on the speed of jaguars (the animal)		
Information on neuroscience (including other synonyms for it)		
Information on cell mitosis in animals or plants		
Biography info on Alfred Lothar Wegener		
Dates of solar eclipses from 1800 to 1850		

9. At this point, students are ready to do their own searches. As they research, encourage them to support each other when they run up against roadblocks and get frustrated instead of coming to you first.

Item You Need to Find	What search will you use?	Results (How did it work? How could you refine your search? How do you know the information is reliable?)
PowerPoint files about Arctic adaptations		
Information on the use of wind turbines in Denmark		
Energy resources from government websites		
News articles from the *New York Times* about the Large Hadron Collider, built by CERN		
List of the top ten countries that use geothermal energy sources		
Information on sources of geothermal energy in Iceland		
Primary source information from E. O. Wilson's research on ants		

Figure 7.5 Internet Search Scavenger Hunt (reproducible found at www.heinemann.com/products/E08677.aspx)

Lesson 5: Crafting Our Own Informational Stories

Focus Questions: How do we sort and organize all the information we've gathered to prepare for crafting our stories? How do we use what we've learned about informational stories to write our own?

Big Ideas: Scientists sort and organize information they gather before creating informational stories. Engaging and interesting informational stories clearly communicate the key elements to the target audience in a way that is concise and interesting.

Learning Goals: Students will learn how to sort and organize the information they have gathered via their research. They will apply the elements of good informational stories when they craft their own stories.

Materials:

- Class list of the features of good informational stories
- Model informational stories

Recommended Time: Two to three fifty-minute sessions

Note: For this lesson, we assume that students have already collected the information needed to create their own stories.

Lesson:

Sort and Organize

1. Ask students to sort their notes, grouping them by similar ideas. Remind them that note-taking is meant to provide them with a menu of ideas. They may not use every single idea they take a note on, but the notes will help them make choices about how pieces of information will fit together to answer their question.

2. Once they have scanned through and categorized the information, ask students to make an outline, concept map, or graphic organizer showing their question, big idea or message, and the information they're going to include to support it. This will map out the logical sequence of the story. In the case of video or audio stories, students should write a script or a storyboard. At this point, they should ask themselves, *What information do I actually need? What additional information is missing? How can I get it?*

3. After students have created outlines, ask them to share with other students in small groups to get feedback. Here are some questions that they might ask each other:

- Does the outline include information that answers the question?
- Is enough information provided? Too much?
- Does the outline flow logically?
- What other information might be needed to answer the question?

4. Review students' finished outlines and provide additional feedback.

Crafting Informational Stories

1. Before students begin crafting their stories, ask them to revisit their question, purpose, audience, and setting.

2. Review the class list of features of good informational stories. Ask students to explain each one and give examples (to help clarify what their stories need to include). This is a great time to show some student exemplars (perhaps from the previous year) or other model stories that include the elements that you want to see in your students' stories.

3. As students begin to build their stories based on their outlines, remind them to chunk their information into smaller paragraphs. It may help to have students imagine each chunk as a scene in the larger story and visualize what image would help illustrate the important points.

4. Next, students can start to think about how to make their stories engaging and interesting. Have students work on answering the following questions.

- *What visuals will I include?* It's important for students to draft their visuals. These days, it's too common for students to simply pull an image off the Internet without thinking about how the image helps tell the story. We like to have students draw a simple sketch of what an ideal image(s) would be for each section of the story. Then they can either create or find the images.

- *How will I make a personal connection to my audience?* Have students think about what their audience will identify with and how they can make that connection.

- *What voice will I use?* Ask students to decide from whose point of view the story will be told. Will they use a third-person narrator or do something more inventive (like telling the story of a rock from the perspective of the rock)?

- *What will I use to hook my reader into the story?* At the start, we often have students consider how they will hook their audience into their story. It can be helpful to give students time to write their opening hook and share it with other students to get feedback.

- *How can I create suspense?* As students proceed, discuss with them the importance of suspense in a story and have them consider how they can use it to keep their audience engaged.

5. Once students have completed their rough drafts, have them share their stories with each other and give specific feedback on the key elements. The feedback can take a variety of forms:

- *Face-to-face feedback in pairs or small groups:* For this to be successful, students need to feel trusting of each other, but it may also feel safer than sharing with the entire class.

- *Round-robin feedback:* Groups rotate through each other's projects, reading them and giving feedback. To make this option workable from a time standpoint, have students focus on one or two things to give feedback about.

- *Class blog feedback:* Using a class blog to give feedback lets students take more time and write more thoughtful, specific feedback. This is also a great option if you're tight on time during class.

Based on the feedback they receive, students can create their final drafts.

Useful Prompts for Helping Students Craft Science Stories

Question, Problem, Big Idea, Message

- What is the story about?
- What question(s) will the story answer?
- What is the message that I want to get across to my audience?
- What is the big idea?

Title

- How can I convey what the story is about in seven words or less?
- How can I make the title grab the attention of the audience?

Hook

- What is a catchy first sentence that will get the attention of the audience?

Audience

- What example or experience can I use to illustrate that so it will be clear to my audience?

- What will be my audience's reaction to that?

- What comparison can I make that makes that clearer?

- Why does that matter?

- What do I mean by that?

- Why do people need or want to know about it?

- How can the story be broken down so it's easier to understand?

Characters

- Who are the main characters of the story? (Main characters can be people, things, events, or phenomena.)

- What details do we want to know more about? What is its story? What happened to it? How did it change? Why did it change? How was it formed? What might happen in the future? Why?

- What are the characters doing? Why are they doing it? If the characters are people, what are they feeling? Why?

Setting

- Where does the story take place?

- How can I describe the setting vividly so that the audience can see it?

Plot

- What happens next?

- What is the sequence of events or story that are key to answering the question or solving the problem?

- What is the tension in the story?

Evidence

- What's my evidence?

continues

- What evidence should I include to explain the story and show the audience that it's relevant?

Conclusion

- How can I sum up the message and evidence in a way that leaves the audience feeling satisfied?

Visuals

- What visuals can I use to clearly illustrate this idea?

Voice and Grammar

- Who is telling the story? What is his or her perspective?
- What is the tone that I'm trying to set?
- How can I restate that?

Structure

- Does the story flow smoothly?
- Did I include only information that was vital to the message or big idea?

Adapted from Newkirk (2014, 83).

Weaving Informational Stories into Your Teaching

Our purpose for having students create informational stories might be to

- inspire their curiosity and teach them how to find out answers to their questions,
- give them opportunities to go through the process of communicating science information effectively,
- allow them to learn more about a topic after they have conducted their own hands-on inquiry investigations, or
- demonstrate their understanding and ability to synthesize information in new ways.

Above all, we try to make sure the stories are woven seamlessly into the big ideas and practices of science that we already teach. Suggestions for integrating student informational stories into your curriculum are shown in Figure 7.6.

Questions to Ask When Planning	Suggestions
• How will I spark and keep track of student questions that may later be the source of informational stories? • Where are key points where students can gather information to create informational stories on their own (after they have explored on their own as much as they can via hands-on inquiry)? • What authentic audiences can they communicate their informational stories with (the global online audience, their peers, younger students, parents, the school community, the local community)?	• Be strategic about the resources that you provide to students in order to differentiate in subtle ways. We like to provide a range of informational resources for students (at all different levels and media types) so we can guide students to appropriate resources. • Find out what is being taught in science at other grade levels. This may give you clues on potential authentic audiences. For instance, if your eleventh graders are studying ecosystems, maybe they could put together stories for fifth graders who are just being introduced to the concept of the movement of matter among plants, animals, decomposers, and the environment.

Figure 7.6 Integrating informational stories into the curriculum

8 Personal Stories of Science

[W]e are made of stories. I mean, scientists say that human beings are made of atoms, but a little bird told me that we are also made of stories.

—Eduardo Galeano

A Story from Melissa

A few years ago, my colleagues and I launched an interdisciplinary climate change project in which students researched and created their own informational stories. We talked about the research that was happening in biology and earth sciences around global climate change and then invited professors and graduate students from a neighboring university in for a one-day in-house research symposium. The scientists shared their personal stories with students: their backgrounds, interests, and research, which included changes in coral reefs, plants at Walden Pond (compared with Thoreau's notes from his time there), and forest ecology. Then, in small focus groups, our students shared their research with the scientists. The impact that this experience had on students was tremendous; they were able to hear directly from scientists about what they do, the questions they are trying to answer, their struggles, and how their research fits into the larger picture of global climate change. The students were also incredibly empowered when they were able to present their own stories (based on research) to the scientists and ask them questions to find out more.

As Melissa's story points out, science is so much more interesting for students if we tap into the stories of the scientists behind it—their questions, their struggles, and the often-convoluted paths that led them toward their discoveries.

Personal Stories: Getting to Know the People Behind the Science

Personal science stories answer questions like these:

- What drives scientists to explore and investigate the world? What were they like as children? Why did they decide to become scientists?
- What are their questions, and ultimately what are the stories that they create?
- What challenges and fears do scientists have to overcome? How do they do that?
- How do scientists' work, struggles, and discoveries change them?
- How have scientists' ideas about science changed over time and why?

They may be created for a wide array of purposes: to share the sense of wonder that scientists experience, teach others about the people behind the science, highlight the struggles that scientists often have to overcome, give examples of the variety of people who become scientists, demonstrate understanding, or personally reflect on ourselves as scientists or our thoughts about science. They can be about famous scientists, but they are even more intriguing when we delve into the stories of not-so-famous scientists (especially ones in our community and those that students can meet firsthand or through correspondence) and the stories of our students as scientists.

Personal stories also humanize science and connect students to scientists. Some people think that scientists are boring, humorless people who exist mainly to solve equations and talk with their lab-coated colleagues using words that no one else can understand. These perceptions couldn't be further from the truth—as we know, scientists are creative, imaginative people (of all different backgrounds and genders) who work in a variety of exotic places (under the sea, in volcanoes, in labs, on mountaintops, etc.). When people have these misconceptions of scientists, they can't relate to them and therefore have trouble relating to their work.

Also, research shows that when students make personal connections to what they're learning, they're more invested and engaged. Personally connecting to and empathizing with scientists involved in the topics that they're studying may give them a reason to learn the content. If students can get a glimpse of who scientists really are, where they came from, why they're passionate about science, and what challenges they face (and how they overcome them), they will have a more well-rounded knowledge of science and how it works and will become better-informed citizens.

During Melissa's climate change project, students were enthralled when they found out that local scientists were using Henry Thoreau's data from Walden Pond as a baseline for determining possible effects of climate change. In fact, several students volunteered to find out more about Thoreau and his story in order to share it with the rest of the class. One of these stories, excerpts of which are shown here, illustrated the personal connection that the student made to Thoreau and to how his journals are being used for science today.

Henry David Thoreau

It was cold. His boots crunched on the patchy snow as he pulled his coat tighter around him. He could see his cabin just a few yards away, he yearn[ed] for it, but was busy recording nature. A lily had just bloomed, a splash of green and white on barren landscape. He was describing it in detail. Every curve in its leaf, every different color, where and when he saw it and what kind of flower it was.

Oh, I'm sorry! I didn't introduce you to him. This is Henry David Thoreau, writer, philosopher, journalist and scientist (though he didn't know it yet). . . . He loved nature so much that after he graduated from high school, he was mad at his parents for sending him to Harvard College (now Harvard University).

At Harvard, Thoreau became friends with his teacher Ralph Waldo Emerson and became interested in *Transcendentalism, a religious and philosophical movement that believed in the goodness of both people and nature.* This is when Henry's new life began.

Emerson realized Henry's great writing ability and invited him to live [at] his estate on Walden Pond, where the young graduate could devote his time to writing. . . .

He wrote every day and recorded everything! Birds, plants, trees, fish, animals, even the pond itself. . . .

Today, Thoreau's work is greatly admired. His writing skills are superb and his descriptions of plants are so precise that scientists rely on his observations. In fact, they use his notes to identify how climate change impacts nature. This is how it works. Starting in 1851, he began recording the progress of the seasons in Concord, Massachusetts. He noted the arrival of the first flowers and budding leaves, as well as when the migratory birds of the spring arrived. By studying this information, scientists can identify how climate changes has [sic] affected Concord's habitat.

Remember the lily in the beginning of the story? Over the past 160 years, this native flower and roughly a quarter of Concord's wildflowers have been lost, and an additional third have become rare.

How does this happen? Many native flowers are prepared for the cold weather and don't bloom even when it [gets] warm in the spring. Meanwhile, invasive and non-native plants take advantage of the warmer weather and out-compete the native plants.

You might think this is not important. Does it matter if some flowers are never going to grow in Concord again? Absolutely. Slowly, every creature that relies on these plants will also disappear. It will become harder and harder to sustain a balanced environment, and as plants and animals die, human[s] will fall soon after.

Sources

biography.com. N.p., n.d. Web. 7 Jan. 2014. http://www.biography.com/ people/henry-david-thoreau-9506784.

Burleigh, Robert. *A Man Named Thoreau*. Illus. Lloyd Bloom. New York: Atheneum, 1985. Print.

David, Laurie, and Cambria Gordon. *The Down-to-Earth Guide to Global Warming*. New York: Orchard, 2007. Print.

"Henry David Thoreau." *Britannica School*. Encyclopedia Britannica, Inc., n.d. Web. 14 Jan. 2014. http://school.eb.com/levels/middle/article/277337.

Meltzer, Milton. *Henry David Thoreau*. Minnesota: Lerner, 2007. Print.

Roach, Marilynne K. *Down to Earth at Walden*. Boston: Houghton Mifflin Co., 1980. Print.

Lessons for Teaching Students to Create the Personal Stories of Science

Even though informational stories focus on science content and personal stories focus on scientists, they are very similar in how they're crafted. They stem from questions, include the features of effective science stories, and must fit the purpose, audience, and setting. The steps involved in creating personal stories are the same as those for crafting informational stories, as discussed in Chapter 7 and shown in Figure 7.1. The five lessons in this chapter focus on the aspects that are unique to personal stories:

- Lesson 1: Introducing the Personal Stories of Science and Comparing the Features of Scientists

- Lesson 2: What Can We Find Out About Scientists from Their Stories?

- Lesson 3: What Makes a Personal Science Story Exceptional?

Lesson 1: Introducing the Personal Stories of Science and Comparing the Features of Scientists

Focus Questions: Why are the stories behind the scenes of science important? What can we find out about scientists from their personal stories? What characteristics of scientists do we have?

Big Idea: The stories of scientists help us understand what scientists are like, their discoveries, and how they work.

Learning Goal: Students will be introduced to personal science stories and learn why they are important.

Materials:

- Texts and videos about scientists
- Chart paper and markers

Recommended Time: One fifty-minute session

Note: Ideally, this lesson should be done at the beginning of the year. It could be done as a stand-alone lesson or in the context of any content.

Lesson:

1. As a preassessment, have students create a concept map about scientists: What do they do? Where do they work? What are they like? What skills do they use? Have students do this independently, and then compile their ideas as a group. Create a class concept map based on their responses. (At the end of the year, you might ask students to do this activity again or revise their original concept maps. Why and how has their thinking changed?)

2. Ask students to share questions they have about scientists, how they work, and what they are like. Create a chart of all students' questions.

3. Tell a story about how you or someone you know became interested in a topic when he or she saw, heard, or read a story about a scientist. Then ask students to turn and talk about times this may have happened to them. Have volunteers share their ideas with the class.

4. Explain that the class is going to explore the personal stories of science and scientists. These are stories that focus on what scientists do, where they came from, why they're passionate about science, and what their challenges are (and how they overcome them). Assign each pair of students a reading or video about a different scientist. Ask each pair to make a chart of the characteristics of their scientist. Then have each pair join with another pair to form groups of four. Students will share their scientists' stories and features in the new mixed groups. They will add to their original group charts based on their conversations.

5. Facilitate a class discussion: "What do the scientists we learned about have in common? How are they different?" Create a class chart. See Figure 8.1.

6. Ask students to individually reflect on the question, What features of a scientist do I have? and record their thoughts in their science notebooks. (You might have students revisit this reflection at the end of the year and note how their ideas have changed.)

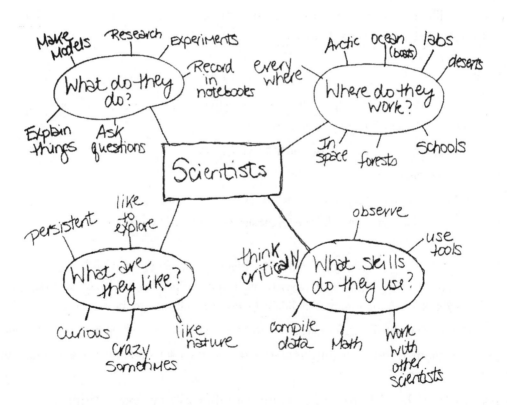

Figure 8.1 Student responses about scientists are compiled in a class chart.

Lesson 2: What Can We Find Out About Scientists from Their Stories?

Focus Question: What can we learn about scientists from their stories?

Big Ideas: We can analyze scientists' stories to find out the questions they asked, their discoveries, the significance of their discoveries, and the struggles they encountered.

Learning Goal: Students will analyze the stories of scientists to identify their questions, discoveries, and struggles.

Materials:

- Model stories about scientists (see Appendix B for suggestions)

Recommended Time: One or two fifty-minute sessions

Notes: In this lesson, you can use one resource (or a differentiated group of resources about the same scientist) for the entire class or resources about several different scientists. If students are researching different scientists, they can share their findings in mixed groups and talk about how their scientists were alike and different.

Lesson:

1. Explain to students that they will be analyzing the personal stories of scientists to learn more about them. The focus questions are

   - What questions were the scientist(s) trying to answer?
   - What discovery did the scientist(s) make?
   - What was the significance of the discovery?
   - What, if any, struggles did the scientist(s) encounter? How did they attempt to overcome them?

2. While students are watching, reading, or listening, ask them to answer the focus questions in their science notebooks. (*Note:* If you are showing a video or listening to a podcast, it is helpful to stop periodically to give students time to make notes.)

3. After students watch, read, or listen, have them share their notes with partners or table groups.

4. Have groups report out highlights of what they learned or found interesting or surprising.

Lesson 3: What Makes a Personal Science Story Exceptional?

Focus Question: What are the features of an exceptional personal science story?

Big Idea: Engaging personal science stories create a personal connection between the audience and the main character and show how the main character changed over time to overcome his or her struggles.

Learning Goal: Students will learn how to identify what makes exceptional personal science stories effective.

Materials:

- Model personal science stories in different forms: book excerpts, videos, podcasts, etc.
- Chart paper and markers

Recommended Time: One to two fifty-minute sessions

Notes: For this activity, it's OK to use personal stories that your students have read, listened to, or watched before (focusing on the content). In this case, they'll be analyzing the stories through a different lens, focusing on the craft of the stories. Also, we find it really helpful to save exemplars of great student science stories from year to year so we can use them in this lesson.

Lesson:

1. Explain that students will be analyzing several personal science stories to find out what elements make them great. They will be taking on the role of story critics and will need to record what they like and don't like about each story and why.

2. Provide an array of different stories at different reading levels and in different media (podcasts, videos, graphic novels, etc.) and allow small groups to pick the stories that they would like to analyze. Give students a recording sheet or ask them to record their thinking in their science notebooks. Ideally, we like to have each group critique at least two to three stories (preferably in different media) and then create a list of the features of an exceptional personal story.

Criteria for Great Personal Science Stories
- Characters we can relate to
- We get emotionally involved
- Good plot (a "ripping" yarn)
- Exciting!
- Interesting info – something we hadn't known before
- Cool visuals
- Suspense
- Descriptions make us feel like we're there
- Vivid language
- Not too long / concise
- Connects to the science we're learning in class
- Easy to understand (no big crazy words or acronyms!)

Figure 8.2 Class chart of the criteria of good personal science stories, which students will use when they create their own stories

3. Pair each group with another group and have them share their findings and their lists. Ask them to come to consensus on what makes a personal science story exceptional; then have them share out with the entire class so that you can create a class list of criteria. (See Figure 8.2 for an example.) Following are some questions to enhance this discussion:

- Are the criteria for a great personal science story similar to or different from the criteria for great explanatory stories and informational stories? How?

- Are the criteria that we came up with similar to what you look for in a really good novel? Why or why not?

Lesson 4: Crafting Personal Science Stories

Focus Question: How can we create effective personal science stories?

Big Ideas: Creating a personal science story involves (1) finding a good question; (2) identifying the story's purpose, audience, and setting; (3) making a plan for gathering information; (4) gathering information; (5) sorting and organizing the information; (6) creating the story; and (7) reflecting on the experience.

Learning Goal: Students will create personal science stories.

Materials:

- Crafting Science Stories Visual (Figure 7.1, page 98)
- Internet resources and research tools, including copies of the Google Search Operators Chart (Figure 7.3, page 103) and the Information Reliability Test (Figure 7.4, page 104)
- Scaffolded Note-Taking Sheets (if needed) (see Figure 8.3)

Recommended Time: Three to four fifty-minute classes

Notes: The process of creating personal science stories is almost identical to that for writing informational stories, just focusing on scientists themselves instead of the science. Instead of repeating the informational story lessons here (Lessons 3, 4, and 5 in Chapter 7), we have created this condensed lesson. If you have already taught your students how to create informational stories, you may want to skip this lesson.

Lesson:

1. Give students an overview of the process of crafting personal stories and share the visual (Figure 7.1) and class chart outlining the process. Post them in the classroom.

2. Ask students to work in pairs to research past and present scientists who worked or are working on the topic that you're currently studying. Each pair should come up with a list of four or five scientists. The list should include brief summaries of what the scientists are or were working on.

3. Have each pair share its initial research with the class. Create a class list of all the scientists and the topics of their work.

4. Ask students to select a scientist that they'd like to find out more about. You may choose to have students work in small groups or individually (depending on your purpose and the comfort level of students for doing this work). More than one student or group can study the same scientist. Having multiple types of stories about the same scientist can show how the same story can be told in many ways.

5. Have each student brainstorm all the questions he or she has about the scientist. Then the student can select one to three questions to be the core of his or her personal science story. (*Note*: Some students may need detailed scaffolding to help them identify questions and take notes as they gather information. The sheet in Figure 8.3 may be helpful).

6. Next, you or the students need to choose the purpose, audience, and setting for their stories and what types of storytelling tools they will use.

7. Now that they have the groundwork set for their stories, students will make plans for their informational research (See Lesson 3 in Chapter 7 for more details, if needed).

8. After their plans are in place, students will gather information for their stories. If needed, review how to use Internet searches effectively and how to find reliable sources (see Lesson 4 in Chapter 7). Hand out copies of the Google Search Operators Chart and the Information Reliability Test if needed.

9. When students have collected their information, ask them to sort and organize it, grouping their notes into like topics. This will help them create their outlines, concept maps, or graphic organizers to map out their stories. It will also point out gaps in their research and what information they still might need to sleuth out.

10. Now students are ready to start crafting their stories—keeping their purpose, audience, setting, and the features of great personal science stories in mind. (See Lesson 5 in Chapter 7.) We suggest having students give each other feedback on their draft stories before they revise them and share them with their audience.

11. Finally, give students the opportunity to reflect on the process of crafting personal stories. What worked well? What do they need to improve on next time?

NAME: _____ DATE: _____

SCIENTIST: _____

Collecting Information About a Scientist

As you gather information about your scientist, please consider the following questions (not meant to be in any particular order). You may not be able to find details for each idea, but see what you can do; the more information you get, the better your story will be.

Questions	Notes
What are the scientist's personal traits? What three words might you choose to describe the scientist and why? (What evidence from his or her life supports those choices?)	
What was the scientist like as a child? Who or what influenced this person?	
Why did this person decide to become a scientist?	
What would you imagine a typical day in the life of your scientist looks like?	
What observations about the world has the scientist made?	

Figure 8.3 Scaffolded Note-Taking Sheet for Gathering Information on Scientists for Personal Stories

Questions	Notes
What questions has the scientist sought to answer?	
What discoveries did the scientist make? What was the impact of these discoveries?	
What challenges or fears did the scientist face or have to overcome in his or her life or work? How did he or she manage to do that?	
How have the scientist's work, struggles, and discoveries molded, shaped, or changed him or her?	
What questions does the scientist still wish to answer? (For living scientists only)	
What else did you learn about the scientist that you found interesting?	
What are two questions you might ask of the scientist?	

(reproducible found at www.heinemann.com/products/E08677.aspx)

Lesson 5: Student Science Memoirs

This lesson was inspired by a lesson created by Ryan Keser, a grades 7–8 science teacher at Lawrence School in Brookline, Massachusetts.

Focus Questions: What are my experiences with science? What are the features of a scientist that I have? How has my thinking about science changed over time? What skills do I need to work on as a scientist?

Big Ideas: Scientists constantly reflect on their experiences, what they have learned, and how they might improve in the future.

Learning Goals: In their notebooks, students will reflect on their background, their science skills, how their ideas about science may have changed, and the science skills that they need to work on in the future. They can use these reflections to improve their science learning in the future.

Materials:

- Science notebooks

Recommended Time: One to two fifty-minute sessions

Lesson:

1. Explain to students that they will be writing science memoirs that describe their experiences with science. Ask students to search their memories for experiences in their past that triggered their curiosity about science—situations or people that encouraged them to ask questions and try to find out the answers.

2. Give students these prompts to consider and ask them to pick one to write as their story:
   - Describe a memorable science moment that you had (e.g., an experience in or out of school that served as an aha moment, made you wonder further, confused you, or inspired you to action).
   - How has your thinking about science changed over time?
   - What features of a scientist do you have? What science skills do you need to work on?

3. Suggest that each student start by listing or creating a concept map of his or her ideas before organizing them. Review the class criteria for exceptional personal science stories and remind students to try to follow them as they create their science memoirs.

PUTTING LESSON 5 INTO ACTION: EXAMPLE MEMOIRS

Following are excerpts from some student memoirs to illustrate how students reflect on their interest in science and themselves as scientists.

Zoe S.

I remember planting seeds with my mom in our garden and watching them grow into vegetables too heavy for me to hold, or looking through a telescope at night at summer camp. Through all of these experiences, I was discovering the world and piecing together knowledge of how it worked.

Kaesha M.

Then came sixth grade, seventh grade, eighth grade. My mind awakened to the wonders of *learning*, old subjects that I found boring were suddenly rich with information. I relearned anatomy, studied things too small for the naked eye to see. Wondered about the depths of the ocean floor. Analyzed what made the wind blow and the snow fall. Tried to understand the workings of what powered our civilization. And then the simpler things I had once taken for granted; what made things stop, start, fall? Everything was a novelty, everything interested me. The fascination that I had suppressed as a child burst forward in full glory.

Naomi M.

I always have had a love of the universe. I thought about how huge it was and how tiny we as humans were—it both horrified yet amazed me, but what I always thought was even more amazing is how inside of each one of us, there are so many tiny particles working together to keep us intact and alive, and how these tiny little cells are so intelligent and how they've developed over time to be able to create a human out of barely nothing, it's just stunned me.

Weaving Personal Stories into Your Teaching

To make personal connections to scientists in our teaching, we feature the stories of scientists who studied or are currently studying the topic we're teaching alongside the content. We've found that this real-world context makes the content much more interesting for students and helps them visualize themselves as scientists when they do investigations that are similar to those professional scientists do. To weave these stories into your teaching, you can tell the stories of scientists and how they made their discoveries (watch movies about scientists, share the background of the scientists behind the science); tell your own science stories (How did you get interested in science? Who inspired you?); and show students your science notebooks and any scientific work that you've done.

Figure 8.4 provides some tips for weaving personal stories into what you already teach.

Questions to Ask When Planning	Suggestions
• Who are the scientists (in the past and present) who are studying these topics or doing this research? • Who are the scientists who made the discoveries? How did they learn what they did? What questions did they have? How do we know what we know? • How can you help students record their thinking about themselves as scientists so they can reflect on what they've learned and how they have grown as scientists?	• Ask students to research the scientists behind the topics they're learning about. Have them peruse current scientific news websites and articles to find out what the cutting-edge discoveries are and who is making them. • Build student reflection into your teaching so students begin to think of themselves as scientists, reflecting on the practices they're using and their characteristics (curiosity, persistence, close observation, etc.), and comparing themselves to the scientists that study the topics in your classroom.

Figure 8.4 Integrating personal stories into the curriculum

Here's an example of how personal stories can be seamlessly added to what you teach. In middle school, students learn about cell division through mitosis. They often wonder, "How do we know the details of this complex process that takes place at such a small scale?" This is an ideal place to bring in the fascinating story of Shinya Inoue, a cell biologist who, despite limited access to labs and materials during World War II, invented the first microscope that could be used to see dynamic processes in cells using polarized light (out of machine gun parts!). As a result of his invention, he and other scientists could observe cells dividing in much more detail.

We have students listen to or watch Inoue's story and take notes using the focus question, How do we know what we know about cells? Then they create personal stories about Inoue based on their notes and additional research (see the following extract). The purpose is to inform the general public about Inoue's discovery and his persistence in the face of difficulties. When students have completed their stories, we have a class discussion about how the tools of science influence the type of evidence we can collect and, as a result, our theories. We use a podcast by Sara Robberson (2012) and a video by *iBioMagazine* (2011) for this project.

Following is an excerpt from a story by one of Melissa's sixth graders.

Shinya Inoue

Shinya Inoue, a Japanese biologist, may not be well known among many people, but many scientists have heard of him. He was a man who contributed much to answering a question that had existed since cells were first studied; why and how do cells divide?

His journey to find this answer began when he was in high school, and Katsuma Dan was his teacher. However, Dan taught in a different way, allowing students much freedom in what they wished to explore. Shinya had looked at a model of nerve conduction, and found the model intriguing, so he decided to study biology.

Later on, he was shown a book by W. J. Schmidt that had a picture of sea urchin eggs. Schmidt had done an observation of these eggs, and first thought the little dots in the eggs were chromosomes, but then decided they were mitotic spindles after more observations. Dan and his students tried to do the same thing Schmidt did, but it didn't succeed. Dan gave Shinya the question that remained unanswered for so long, why and how cells divide. Dan thought that the mitotic spindles were responsible for cell division. Then World War II came, and even though it was pretty dangerous, Shinya believed that one still needs to live despite war, so he continued to work on finding the answer.

After World War II, Shinya built a microscope to help him see the cells clearer. He saw that the spindle of a cell is not just fixed, but dynamic, meaning it changes, and one of the causes is heat. He also made a theory that molecules falling apart can create pulling forces, and this took 20 years to be proven correct. Then, after some more research, Shinya Inoue found the answer to this question, and hoped that it could be used to cure diseases and prevent problems from happening due to the cell division.

Shinya Inoue contributed a lot to biology, and this was from his dedication to it. Many scientists look up to him as a model for what he did and what he found out. That is the story of Shinya Inoue.

This student did a good job of transferring what she learned about Shinya Inoue into story form. We would ask the student to consider the following questions during the revision process: How might the story read through the eyes of the audience? What vocabulary related to cells and cell division needs to be defined or explained (e.g., *nerve conduction* and *mitotic spindles*)? How does the setting impact this story? (World War II is raging and yet Inoue, single-minded in his purpose, continues to work to answer a central question that had eluded scientists for decades.) We would encourage the student to slow down and show the audience what this looks like—that is, provide details to help readers see, hear, and feel what a day in the life of Shinya Inoue must have been like at this time in this particular setting. More detail about the kind of personal traits Inoue must have had in order to carry on his work in the midst of a dangerous war would help strengthen this story further.

We would also encourage the student to experiment with different leads. One way to hook the reader might be to open the story with a scene from the concentration camp where Inoue was living and where he ultimately managed to build from junk parts the microscope that would lead to the answer about how cells divide.

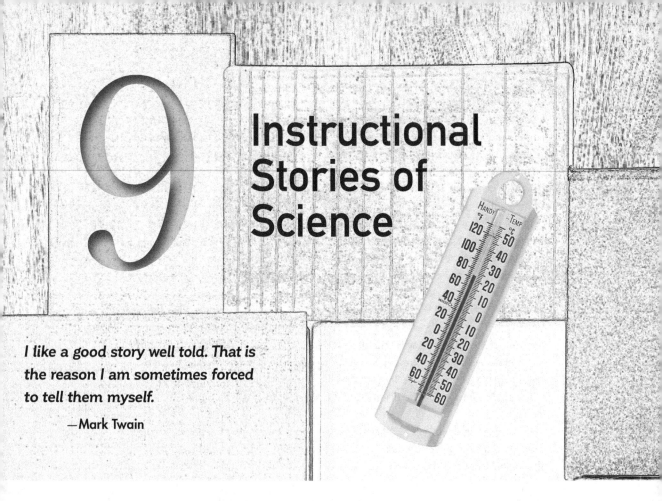

9 Instructional Stories of Science

I like a good story well told. That is the reason I am sometimes forced to tell them myself.

—Mark Twain

A Story from Melissa

After several years of teaching our three sixth-grade science units (water, electricity, and the central nervous system), I had an epiphany. It suddenly made perfect sense how these units were connected. The answer lay in the electrons, of course! We started by looking at the world of atoms and atomic particles to see how water is built and why the polarity of the water molecule (which is related to its electrons) affects its properties. Then we moved on to how similar properties relate to magnets, and from there it was a natural progression first to electricity and then to how electrical impulses take place in the brain and nervous system. Making these connections and being able to put sixth-grade science concepts in the form of a cohesive story line made learning much more meaningful (and a lot more fun!) for my students.

So far in this book, we've focused on teaching students how to craft science stories and effectively communicate them to their audience. In this chapter, we zoom out and highlight a fourth type of story that is just for teachers: the instructional stories of science. These stories allow us to shape our teaching around science big ideas and frame learning in a larger-scale context at several levels. We can craft story lines that tie all units in a grade level together (like Melissa did) and story lines that make the units themselves coherent. Here we share our experiences on how to create instructional stories at both the grade and the unit level, as well as provide details on how to weave specific types of student stories into them.

Framing the Learning with Coherent Story Lines

As we mentioned in Chapter 1, stories can be compelling vehicles for connecting people to information. When we create overarching story lines for instruction (within a unit, throughout a year of study, or over several years), students are more likely to remember what we teach. Information is more likely to stick because (as cognitive science shows) stories are the basic organizing principle for memory. Compelling stories also engage more of the brain (Berns et al. 2013). Also, students can begin to see the big ideas of science and how they connect across disciplines. Finally, the story lines give students a coherent framework to hang their learning on.

A Story Line Across the Year

We like to frame science instruction for each grade level not in terms of the topics, but in terms of the title, if you will, for that year's story line. For instance, in grade 8, we use the title "Spaceship Earth"—the story of Earth's place in the solar system and the interactions between all the players (astronomy), the forces behind those interactions (physics), and what everything in the universe is made of (chemistry). The cross-cutting concept for this year of study is systems.

At the beginning of the year, we typically share the year's science story outline with students so they can begin to think about the context for their learning. We do this verbally and often visually (with a colorful chart hung in the classroom outlining the "road map" for the year). Throughout the year, we refer to where we are on the road map and point out repeatedly how what students are learning about fits into the story. For example, "Why are we learning about diffusion? Diffusion is the process that allows molecules (like food and waste) to move in and out of the body's cells, so it's critical to all living things and is part of what it means to be alive." At the end of the year, we like to have students create their own visual representations showing their interpretations of what they learned and how it all fits together. In essence, they are creating informational stories of their learning. If they add how their thinking has changed, the stories could be both informational and personal.

A Story Line Within a Unit

An example of a story line that we use for a specific unit (the central nervous system) begins with the idea of body systems (What are they and why are they so different in various animals? Why did these different body systems evolve? How are they different from human body systems?). This leads to a study of human body systems, and then we embark on a detailed study of the central nervous system (the control center for all of the body systems)—the parts, what they do, and how they all work together—relating this all to the students themselves (What's happening in your body and nervous system when you're frightened? Nervous?). Finally, students research substances that affect the health and function of the brain (drugs, alcohol, etc.).

Uncovering Your Instructional Stories: A Yearlong Story Line Example

The process of creating instructional story lines does not involve revamping your curriculum. Instead, it's a thoughtful way of looking for connections between the topics you already teach— connecting them through story. We find that teaching using story lines also makes it much more interesting for us.

Creating instructional stories is very much the same as the process for creating informational and personal stories (with a few tweaks):

1. *Find a Question:* How can you create instructional story lines for your units and years of study?

2. *Identify Purpose, Audience, and Setting:* The purpose of creating instructional story lines is to deepen student understanding, make vital connections between the content visible for students (the audience), and create a coherent curriculum in your classroom (the setting).

3. *Make a Plan:* What information will you need and how will you gather it? Who will be involved in doing this work and when will it be done? What's the time frame and schedule for completion? Will it be shared with others? If so, how?

4. *Gather Information:* Collect information on the topics you will teach, applicable standards, big ideas, essential questions, crosscutting concepts, and science and engineering practices before creating an instructional story.

5. *Sort and Organize the Information:* By sorting and organizing the information, you can identify connections and draft outlines or storyboards of possible story lines.

6. *Create the Story (and Put It into Action):* Using the outline or storyboard, create the story and infuse it into your lesson plans.

7. *Reflect:* Keeping track of what worked and what didn't work will help you refine the story for next time.

In the following sections, we describe these steps, using examples from our seventh-grade curriculum to illustrate how it works. We begin with step 3 since the first two steps are fairly generic when creating instructional stories.

This process can be done individually or as a team. Sometimes we start individually and then share our ideas with others to fine-tune them.

Making a Plan

When crafting instructional stories, we've learned the hard way that it's best to have a plan. The first time we did this, we just winged it. We eventually got to where we wanted to be, but it took a long time and we took several wrong turns along the way. We suggest thinking carefully about the specific steps that you'll take, such as what specific information and materials you'll need and how will you get them. You'll also need to clearly map out the logistics. Who will do this work, when will it happen, and what are the deadlines?

When we crafted the seventh-grade story line, which we built from a collection of discrete geology, cell, and evolution units, we made a list of all the information we needed and who would gather it. We also asked participants to think about possible essential questions, big ideas, crosscutting concepts, and science and engineering practices beforehand to jump-start our work together. The plan was for a small team of five to six teacher volunteers to do this work in one day.

Gathering Information

When you begin thinking about instructional story lines, take a close look at the topics that you already teach and gather key information that will help you develop story lines. Questions to ask as you pull together this information include the following:

- *What are the topics you teach?*
- *What are the state standards behind them?* The standards may help you decide which big ideas to focus on or how to connect topics.

- *What big ideas capture the essence of these topics?* The Disciplinary Core Ideas in the Next Generation Science Standards (available at http://ngss.nsta.org/DisciplinaryCoreIdeasTop.aspx) will help you identify these.

- *Are there specific science and engineering practices and crosscutting concepts that come to the forefront when teaching these topics that may be used to tie the content together?* The Next Generation Science Standards (NGSS) and the *Framework for K–12 Science Education* (Committee on a Conceptual Framework for New K–12 Science Education Standards 2012; see www.nextgenscience.org/framework-k–12-science-education) provide information on concepts and practices that we can use to tie the big ideas together.

- *What essential questions do you want students to grapple with that might be big enough to frame the year, the unit, or major parts of the unit?*

Sorting and Connecting Information

Now that you have all of the information in front of you, you're ready to start the messy but rewarding process of thinking about possible story lines. First of all, brainstorm possible connections between all of these topics (we like to do this with colleagues, putting our collective brainpower to work!). Some people like to begin by grouping the topics together around the big ideas. Others like to start with key essential questions that then lead to the big ideas.

This is where we get out the markers and chart paper and create concept maps. (Sometimes we also like to use sticky notes or index cards and tape because we can easily rearrange them.) But you can use any materials that spark your thinking and creativity. The important thing is that you get your ideas down—the big ideas, practices, crosscutting concepts, and any other story ideas that you might have. Then draw arrows between them to show connections. Regroup if necessary and fine-tune. Notice all the arrows (they will help map out where to make connections in the curriculum later). (See Figure 9.1.)

This process can be messy at times. We often have some prickly discussions, but they lead us to a much greater understanding of what we want students to walk away with and how we can get them there.

Organizing the Story

OK, so you have some great ideas about the big ideas, essential questions (perhaps), and all the connections that you might make. What's next? Now is the time to think through the lens of your students to begin to organize your story. Where should the story start? If students don't have any knowledge of this topic, where would you need to begin? What are the foundational

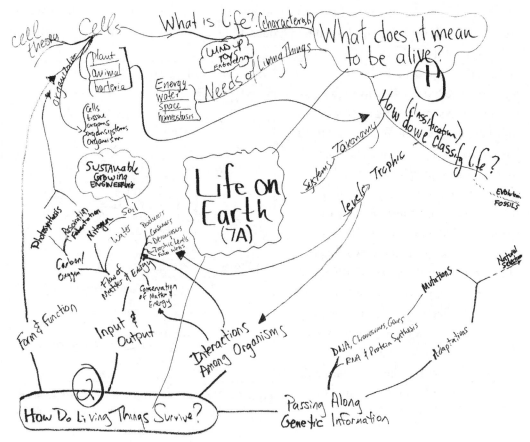

Figure 9.1 Concept maps helped us sort and organize the big ideas, crosscutting concepts, and essential questions to create our seventh-grade instructional story. (This is a final version of one of them; there were a lot of really messy versions before this!)

ideas that you'll be building on? How should the plot develop? What might students need to know next? Thinking in this stepwise fashion, you can create a storyboard (this can be a visual map, list, outline, etc.). Don't be afraid to revise, revise, revise. (We often go through many drafts before landing on a story that feels just right.) Keep in mind that there may be many possible outlines for the same topics (and that's just fine!). Sometimes we create several different possible story lines and then share the results.

Now, what is the story that fits this sequence? How will you connect the topics in a meaningful way that makes sense for students? What really intriguing questions will you ask to spark their thinking and help them generate their own questions?

In our seventh-grade example, we started with a list of all the science topics we teach: cells, needs of living things, classification, flow of matter and energy in ecosystems, adaptations, evolution, changes in Earth's surface over time, geologic time, plate tectonics, Earth's structure, and so on. Then we categorized them into groups, thinking of how we could teach these topics in the form of story. What are the over-arching themes that pull all of this together? The topics naturally segregate into life science and geology, but what do they have in common? What could be the basis of a yearlong story that encompasses these two big topics? Then we realized that when we zoomed way out, all of the seventh-grade topics were about Earth, specifically life on Earth and Earth's history. The beauty of these two chapters of the seventh-grade story of Earth is that there are so many connections between them! What happens to Earth ultimately affects life and vice versa. This allows us to continuously weave the life science and geology concepts together throughout the year. See Figure 9.2 for the outline we devised to create our story line.

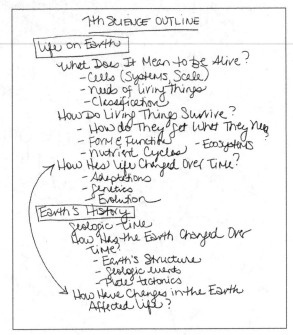

Figure 9.2 The outline of the seventh-grade science story line that we used to craft the instructional story

Creating and Using the Story

From your outline or storyboard, you can craft the story line. Here's our story line for seventh grade:

> What does it mean to be alive? All living things are made of cells, which are made of parts that work together as a system. Living things have certain things that they need to survive (water, source of energy, space, air). They get what they need to survive in different ways, according to their role in ecosystems and affected by the form and function of their structures and parts. The types and forms of life on Earth have changed over time in order to adapt to changes in the environment.
>
> Earth has changed significantly over its 4.5 billion years because of plate tectonics, major geologic events, and the forces of weathering and erosion. These changes in Earth itself have driven the changes in life on Earth. As a result, the geologic history and the history of life on Earth are closely intertwined. Throughout this story of our planet, crosscutting themes emerge: systems, nutrient cycles, and energy, in addition to the idea that Earth is constantly changing.

After you create your story line, you can organize your lessons and resources to match the story. How and when will you segue between topics? Where will you circle back to a topic you taught before to bring it into new context for students and help them build their knowledge? The arrows on the concept maps that you created (like the one shown in Figure 9.1) will show you where these connections and spiraling can occur. If you post concept maps in the classroom (or create them together as a class and have students add to them as you go along), the connections between topics will naturally become part of teaching and learning in your classroom.

Reflecting

When you try out the story line, be sure to take notes on what works well and what doesn't. This information will be helpful in improving your story next year. We've found that sometimes there are important pieces of information missing that students need as a foundation. Or maybe the flow of the story really doesn't make sense after all; for example, perhaps it would have made more sense to talk about form and function before adaptations (or vice versa). Any time students seem to get hung up or can't make the connections that we'd hoped they could, it raises a red flag. We know we need to modify the story line.

We've found that structuring our teaching around a yearlong cohesive story, and sharing that story with students, helps students see the big picture instead of getting caught up in the nitty-gritty facts and details that support the big ideas. Instead of marching straight through the topics we need to teach, we constantly circle back to ideas, refining student understanding of what they already learned and adding to that knowledge within the structure that the story line creates. This leads to deeper student understanding and much more interesting student questions, some of which develop as we think about how all the big ideas fit together.

Creating an Instructional Story Line for Water: A Unit Example

The same process that we described for creating instructional stories for a year of study can be used for individual units.

Water is a major topic of study for us in sixth grade. When we thought about the ultimate story we wanted our students to be able to tell about water on Earth by the end of the unit, we decided an important place to begin was by asking them a simple question: "Where does water hide on Earth?" Just the word *hide* was enough to invite students to consider the fact that water abounds not just in the obvious places (oceans, rivers, ponds, and lakes) but also in places we cannot see so easily and therefore might have a tendency to overlook (underground, the atmosphere, living things, and ice sheets and glaciers). We realized that this simple question—and its follow-up, "How does water move on Earth?"—framed much of the learning we knew students would undertake throughout the unit.

Our water story begins by focusing on the physical properties of water: strong cohesive force, adhesion to other materials, surface tension, capillary action, high specific heat, and the notion of water as the universal solvent. Students do an introductory hands-on lesson using pipettes and a variety of different materials and surfaces to investigate how water behaves. They also have a chance to explore how some other liquids behave on these same surfaces in order to have some points of reference. We then move into a discussion of water on an atomic level, how the structure of the molecule results in it being slightly polar, and what being a polar molecule means in terms of the way water interacts with water and with molecules of other substances.

Once students understand why water does what it does, we explore the implications on a global scale—Earth's global water cycle. In the last few years, we have been impressed with our students' ability to make the connection from the focus on water at the molecular level and its unique physical characteristics to the much broader global story of water on Earth—the water cycle, or hydrological cycle. When they talk about condensation now, they are able to do more than simply define it as "water vapor turning into liquid." Many of them can explain that condensation results when water vapor molecules lose heat energy, which causes them to slow down. Because of water's strong cohesive force between and among the water molecules, liquid water forms.

The water cycle then naturally transitions into a study of the role of the oceans in climate and weather and a deeper study of the ocean system itself (a natural segue into our ocean systems unit).

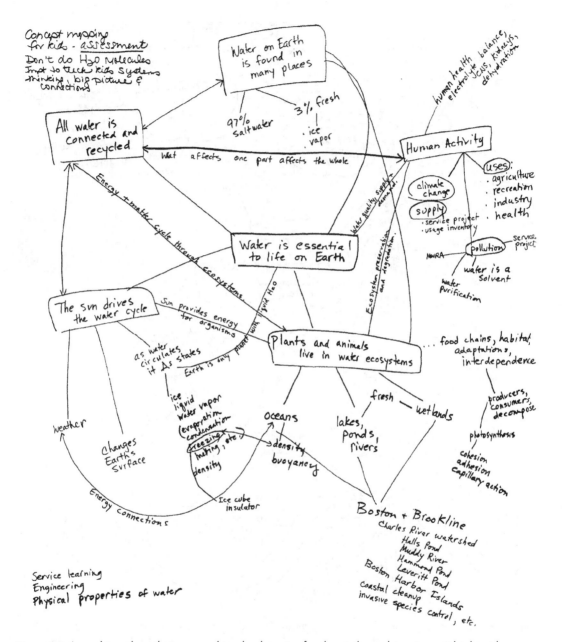

The handwritten concept map contains the following text:

Concept mapping for kids - assessment
Don't do H₂O Molecules
Impt to teach kids systems thinking, big picture & connections

Water on Earth is found in many places
97% saltwater
3% fresh
· ice
· vapor

All water is connected and recycled

What affects one part affects the whole

human health balance, electrolytes, kidneys, dehydration

Human Activity
climate change
supply
· service project
· usage inventory
uses:
· agriculture
· recreation
· industry
· health
MWRA
pollution
service project
water is a solvent
water purification

Energy + matter cycle through ecosystems

Water is essential to life on Earth

Water quality supply demand
Ecosystem preservation and degradation

The sun drives the water cycle
Sun provides energy for organisms

as water circulates it △s states
Earth is only planet with liquid H₂O

Plants and animals live in water ecosystems
... food chains, habitat, adaptation, interdependence
producers, consumers, decompose
photosynthesis
cohesion adhesion capillary action

ice liquid vapor water evaporation (evaporation, condensation, freezing, melting, etc.)
density
Ice cube insulator

oceans
density
buoyancy

lakes, ponds, rivers
fresh — wetlands

weather
changes Earth's surface

Energy connections

Boston + Brookline
Charles River watershed
Halls Pond
Muddy River
Hammond Pond
Leveritt Pond
Boston Harbor Islands
coastal cleanup
invasive species control, etc.

Service learning
Engineering
Physical properties of water

Figure 9.3 A working chart that we used to chunk topics for the sixth-grade water unit by big ideas and to show connections between topics

Figure 9.4 A preliminary map of the entire sixth-grade curriculum (except for the ocean systems unit, which wasn't part of the curriculum when we did this map) framed around the story "Water: The Essence of Life"

Weaving Student Stories into Your Instructional Story Line

Now that you have a sense of what your overarching instructional story line might be for the year and each unit, let's think about where student stories come into play. When we look for places to bring student science stories into our curriculum, we always ask ourselves: *What is our purpose for using science stories or having students create their own science stories? How do the stories support the science content and practice learning goals?* Our purpose may be to have students do any of the following:

- get excited about and actively engage in the content
- generate questions
- deepen their thinking
- craft explanations and be able to critique the explanations of others (explanatory stories)
- research and effectively communicate science information to various audiences (informational stories)
- share the personal stories of science
- demonstrate their understanding
- communicate their ideas in writing or orally

Initially, we scan through the curriculum to find entry points for student stories and think about what our purpose for each specific story might be. We can't weave student stories into each lesson, so where will it provide the most impact to add them in?

When you begin thinking about using science stories, we suggest that you take a close look at your curriculum to identify where you already incorporate the foundations of different types of stories. Do you already ask students to create informational research reports? Perhaps you just need to work more on the effective features of science stories with your students or on having them focus more on purpose and audience. Or maybe you'd like to dig more deeply into explanations at the start, making sure students understand the parts of explanations and how to communicate them effectively.

Remember that you don't have to tackle all types of stories at once! Pick a type of story that is highest on your list and work on that first. The chart in Figure 9.5 can help you start to think about how to include student stories in your curriculum.

Type of Story	Where We Might Incorporate It into the Curriculum
Explanatory stories	• Fit short, informal explanations in whenever students are doing hands-on inquiry or making claims based on other types of data. • Longer, more detailed explanations are best used at key points where students have had many opportunities to gather data to answer a question that focuses on a pivotal big idea. These explanations require them to synthesize information and can be used for assessment.
Informational stories	• Short informational stories can be used throughout the year when students have burning questions that they'd like to answer. • Longer, more detailed informational stories can be built into units as performance assessments (perhaps asking students to summarize what they've learned for an authentic audience). • Informational stories that require in-depth research can be required once or twice a year. This usually works best when you can have each student (or small group of students) research a specific topic (all around one focus question or big idea). Then students can share their stories with one another.
Personal stories	• Share intriguing stories about scientists that connect to the topics being taught anytime. • At least once in a unit, give students the chance to research the scientists behind the science and create personal stories. If you want to use these stories to engage students in the topic, you can assign this activity at the beginning of the unit. Otherwise, you can integrate the student stories within the unit or at the end (if you want to have students research the scientists on their own and craft stories of one that they are most interested in). • Student memoirs can be crafted at the beginning of the year and again at the end of the year. Then students can reflect on how their science thinking and skills have changed, what they learned, and what further questions they have. (You could also do this at the beginning and end of a unit.)

Figure 9.5 Quick reference guide to weaving the stories of science into the curriculum

Your Turn!

Now that we've starting doing this, we can't stop thinking in terms of stories. We see them everywhere we turn (and hope that our students will begin to as well). Most importantly, we believe that our work with science stories has really made a difference in teaching our students how to be effective science communicators. We wish you well on your adventures in storytelling!

Science Talk Planning Sheet

Grade:_____ Date:_____

Unit/Lesson:_____ Author:_____

What is the purpose for the science talk?
Focus/overarching question:
Subquestions that will help guide students toward the focus/overarching question:
What science, engineering, and/or nature of science big ideas are you focusing on?

continues

What will students be doing before and after the science talk? Where will it be used in the lesson/unit and inquiry learning cycle?

What are some skills that you need to review/practice with your students prior to the science talk?

How will you set/review the norms with students?

How will you summarize student ideas and ask them to reflect on the ideas that surfaced during the science talk?

In what ways do you want students to record data from the science talk (such as a sociogram)?

Science Talk Prompts

I think _____ because _____.

In my opinion, _____ because _____.

I observed _____ when _____.

I disagree with that idea because _____.

I understand what you said, but I think _____.

I'm not sure about what _____ said because _____.

I hear you saying that _____.

I have a similar idea to _____.

I agree with that idea because _____.

I want to add to what _____ is saying.

I have a question about _____.

I wonder why _____.

How would this be different if _____?

What would happen if _____?

I think this may have happened because _____.

Based on my results and what other people have said, I think _____.

Explanatory Stories
(* = also informational stories)

Resource	Suggested Grade Range	Description
Biology Letters articles (http://rsbl.royalsocietypublishing.org)	9–12	Short, current research articles on many biological science topics.
Scientific American articles (www.scientificamerican.com) and *60-Second Science* podcasts (www.scientificamerican.com/podcast/60-second-science/)*	6–12	Well-written summaries and podcasts of explanations based on scientific articles from scientific journals.
Science articles (www.sciencemag.org)	9–12	Scientific research articles and shorter summaries (in "Letters" and "In Brief" sections).
Nature articles (www.nature.com) and thirty-minute podcasts (www.nature.com/nature/podcast/)	9–12	Scientific research articles (in written and audio format).
The Atlantic articles by Ed Yong (www.theatlantic.com/author/ed-yong/)	6–12	Great examples of explanation stories clearly written by science writer Ed Yong and accompanied by powerful visuals.
Newsela articles (https://newsela.com)*	6–12	Engaging, well-written science stories (explanatory, informational, and personal) on current topics with intriguing visuals. Articles are available in five reading levels, allowing seamless differentiation in the classroom.
Science News (http://sciencenews.org) and *Science News for Students* (www.sciencenewsforstudents.org) articles*	6–12	Well-crafted explanations based on current research on a wide range of topics.
Journal of Emerging Investigators articles (www.emerginginvestigators.org)	6–12	Scientific articles written by middle and high school students.
What If? by Randall Munroe (2014)	6–12	Logical explanations based on data to answer lots of off-the-wall science questions.

Informational Stories
(* = also personal stories; † = also explanatory stories)

Resource	Suggested Grade Range	Description
Books		
A Short History of Nearly Everything, by Bill Bryson (2005)*	6–12	Short essays about almost every science topic under the sun, from the solar system and the universe to atoms to life on Earth. In addition to well-written snippets on science topics (informational stories), Bryson effortlessly weaves in the personal stories of science (and a few explanatory stories as well). We consider this volume to be one of the best resources we have for pulling out short readings on a myriad of topics to engage students in the topics and show them what supreme science storytelling can be.
A Really Short History of Nearly Everything, by Bill Bryson (2009)	6–8	Just like the title implies, this condensed and more visual version of Bryson's *A Short History of Nearly Everything* has even more bite-size informational story chunks. Designed for younger readers, this is a really nice source of readings for text sets (designed to be accessible for all reading levels). The scientific big ideas jump out at the reader and the engaging visuals are very effective.
Phineas Gage, by John Fleischman (2002)	6–12	The spellbinding story of Phineas Gage, the railroad construction foreman who had a thirteen-pound iron rod shot through his brain during a construction explosion in 1848. Phineas survived and became a classic medical case study that allowed doctors to learn about the brain and how it works.
The Violinist's Thumb, by Sam Kean (2012)*	9–12	Using the effective features of science stories masterfully, Sam Kean relates the secrets of our genetic code and the scientists who have been instrumental in the field of genetics.
The Disappearing Spoon, by Sam Kean (2010)*	9–12	Intriguing tales about the elements—their role in history, the people who discovered them, and much more. This book brings fun and life into learning about the periodic table!
Death by Black Hole, by Neil deGrasse Tyson (2007)	9–12	Interesting series of essays about almost everything but the cosmic kitchen sink written in an easily understood way for a general audience by master storyteller Neil deGrasse Tyson (astrophysicist at the American Museum of Natural History).

continues

The Forest Unseen, by David George Haskell (2012)	9–12	Lyrical synopsis of what happens in one square meter of old-growth Tennessee forest over a year as biologist David George Haskell observes and tells its story.
World Without Fish, by Mark Kurlansky (2014)	6–12	Appealing illustrated account of the status of the world oceans and the creatures that live in it. Great for struggling readers; each chapter includes a graphic novel summary.
Under New England, by Charles Ferguson Baker (2008)	6–12	Beautifully illustrated chronicle that explains the geology of New England using colorful analogies and language that is easy for students to understand.
Sea Change, by Sylvia A. Earle (1995)*	9–12	The saga of Sylvia Earle's personal story of exploring the ocean deep is interwoven with informational stories of the intricate connections between what's happening to the world ocean and its inhabitants.
The Soul of an Octopus, by Sy Montgomery (2015)*	9–12	Intriguing exploration into the intelligence and nature of the octopus via the personal stories of the author.
Tracking and the Art of Seeing, by Paul Rezendes (1999)	9–12	Very well crafted field guide with superb photos and illustrations that bring the world of tracking animals to life for the reader.
Winter World, by Bernd Heinrich (2003)	6–12	Enchanting look at the ingenious ways that animals have adapted to survive during the harsh winter with charming hand-drawn sketches throughout. The author's natural wonder and love of nature clearly shine through.
Your Inner Fish, by Neil Shubin (2009)	9–12	Detailed and intriguing story of how we can use evolutionary biology to explain the human body and how it got that way.
Picture Books		
Sea Soup, by Mary M. Cerullo (2001)	6–12	Beautifully illustrated story packed with information about zooplankton that is perfectly written to grab students' attention and give them key details in very readable text.
Moonbird, by Phillip Hoose (2012)	6–12	Inspiring account of a small eastern shore bird who was banded in 1995—its migration patterns, life cycle, and adaptations for survival.
Podcasts		
Quirks and Quarks with Bob McDonald (www.cbc.ca/radio/quirks)	6–12	Great source of science podcasts (it's been on the air for over forty years!).

Podcasts		
Radiolab (www.radiolab.org)	6–12	Thirty-minute audio stories that weave sound, music, and expert interviews together on a variety of science topics.
Science Friday (www.npr.org /podcasts/381444525 /science-friday)[*][†]	6–12	Host Ira Flatow interviews scientists and inventors on a multitude of topics to reveal entertaining and educational informational stories.
The Naked Scientists (www. thenakedscientists.com /podcasts/naked-scientists)	6–12	One-hour informative and funny BBC podcasts feature science news, answers to listeners' questions, and interviews with scientists.
DVDs		
Cosmos (2014)[*]	6–12	Enthralling thirteen-part series, hosted by astrophysicist Neil deGrasse Tyson, about the mysteries of our cosmos and how we know what we do about it. Beautiful visuals and animations.
Planet Earth (2011)	6–12	Outstanding mix of oral narration with stunning videos that captivate viewers and give them glimpses of unforgettable creatures and places.
Data and Photographs		
AAAS Data Stories entries (www.sciencemag.org /projects/data-stories/finalists)	6–12	Finalists of the AAAS Data Stories competition—videos selected for their creativity, complexity, and clarity.
13pt Information Graphics (http://13pt.com/graphics/)	6–12	Gallery of examples from the studio of Jonathan Corum, an information designer and science graphics editor at the *New York Times*. Great examples of infographics (some of which are interactive) that effectively illustrate and explain science concepts.
Science images from *The Telegraph* (www.telegraph .co.uk/news/science /picture-galleries)	6–12	Striking and varied array of science images that tell visual stories.
NSF *Science360 News* pictures of the day (https://news.science360.gov /files/pic-day)	6–12	National Science Foundation's gallery of dazzling science images.

continues

Nature's "365 Days: The Best Science Images of 2015" (www.nature.com/news /365-days-the-best-science -images-of-2015-1.19017)	6–12	*Nature's* collection of jaw-dropping photos from 2015.

Websites		
New York Times "Science" section (www.nytimes.com /section/science)	6–12	Brilliant science stories that are very well written with vivid visuals on a variety of topics.
Newsela (https://newsela .com)†	6–12	Current science news articles available at different reading levels.

Personal Stories
(* = also informational stories)

Resource	Suggested Grade Level	Description
Books		
Never Cry Wolf, by Farley Mowat (1963)*	6–12	Farley Mowat's account of the time he spent in the subarctic regions of Canada as a biologist studying wolves and caribou is a striking personal story as well as an insightful glimpse into the habits and behaviors of wolves.
Letters to a Young Scientist, by Edward O. Wilson (2013)	6–12	A collection of autobiographical personal stories by famed entomologist E. O. Wilson in which he shares his contagious passion for science and solving the wonders of the world.
The Map That Changed the World, Simon Winchester (2001)	9–12	The story of William Smith, a British surveyor who discovered that he could identify rock layers by the unique fossils they held (the Theory of Faunal Succession).
Nature's Machines, by Deborah Parks (2005)	6–12	Fascinating biography of Mimi Koehl, a biomechanist (scientist who uses engineering and physics to study the designs of living things and how they live and move). This book is part of the Women's Adventures in Science series; we recommend the other titles also.

Life on Earth—and Beyond, by Pamela S. Turner (2008)	6–12	A close look at the life and work of astrobiologist Dr. Chris McKay, who researches extreme environments on Earth that resemble those on other planets in order to determine if life can exist on other planets.
Lab Girl, by Hope Jahren (2016)	9–12	Beautifully written memoir of a woman scientist, chronicling the stories of her love of science and nature from her childhood in rural Minnesota through her professional work on plants (she's currently a geobiologist studying fossil plants). Poetic informational stories about plants are interwoven throughout the book.
Longitude, by Dava Sobel (1995)	9–12	The riveting story of how English clockmaker John Harrison solved the century-old problem of measuring longitude. (Before then, sailors could easily measure latitude, but their inability to determine their east–west position caused untold shipwrecks).
Tracking Trash, by Loree Griffin Burns (2007)*	6–12	The fascinating chronicles of oceanographer Dr. Curtis Ebbesmeyer, who tracks trash in the ocean in order to find out about ocean currents and the effects of ocean debris on marine life, as well as the science behind his work.
Digging for Bird-Dinosaurs, by Nic Bishop (2000)	6–12	Account of paleontologist Cathy Foster as she searches for fossils that may link dinosaurs and birds. This book is part of the Scientists in the Field series, all of which are recommended.
Graphic Novels		
Thomas Edison and the Lightbulb, by Scott Welvaert (2007)	6–12	A good example of a graphic novel that tells an effective story using vivid illustrations and enticing text. We also recommend other titles in this Inventions and Discovery series, including *Marie Curie and Radioactivity,* by Connie Colwell Miller (2007), *Louis Pasteur and Pasteurization,* by Jennifer Fandel (2007), and *Isaac Newton and the Laws of Motion,* by Andrea Gianopoulos (2007).
Online Resources		
Secret Lives of Scientists and Engineers (www.pbs.org/wgbh/nova/blogs/secretlife/)	6–12	Short videos (up to three minutes) and short posts about the personal side of scientists (what they do outside the lab and how it relates to their work).

continues

Scientists @ the Smithsonian (www.smithsonianeducation.org/scientist/)	6–12	Short interviews (three to four minutes) with Smithsonian scientists about what they do and where they work.
"Profiles of Scientists and Engineers," NSF *Science 360 Video* (https://science360.gov/series/profiles-scientists-engineers/711d5cab-8416-40f7-9297-099c1f37a9bd)	6–12	Short downloadable videos about a variety of young scientists and engineers
The Stories Behind the Science (www.storybehindthescience.org)	9–12	Well-written stories about a variety of science topics and the scientists behind them, available as printable pdfs (each about four pages long). Topic categories include astronomy, biology, physics, geology, and chemistry.

REFERENCES

Arya, Diana Jaleh, and Andrew Maul. 2012. "The Role of the Scientific Discovery Narrative in Middle School Science Education: An Experimental Study." *Journal of Educational Psychology* 104 (4): 1022–32. doi:10.1037/a0028108.

Bai, Nina. 2011. "Ferry Tale: Fire Ants Aggregate to Living Rafts to Escape Floods." *Scientific American*, April 26. www.scientificamerican.com/article/ferry-tale-fire-ants-can/.

Barker, Charles Ferguson. 2008. *Under New England: The Story of New England's Rocks and Fossils*. Lebanon, NH: University Press of New England.

Berkeley Library. 2016. "Evaluating Resources." August 16. Regents of the University of California. www.lib.berkeley.edu/TeachingLib/Guides/Internet/Evaluate.html.

Berns, Gregory S., Kristina Blaine, Michael J. Prietula, and Brandon E. Pye. 2013. "Short- and Long-Term Effects of a Novel on Connectivity in the Brain." *Brain Connectivity* 3 (6): 590–600. doi:10.1089/brain.2013.0166.

Biography.com editors. 2016. "Jacques Cousteau Biography." Biography.com, January 5. www.biography.com/people/jacques-cousteau-9259496.

Bishop, Nic. 2000. *Digging for Bird-Dinosaurs: An Expedition to Madagascar*. Boston: Houghton Mifflin.

Burns, Loree Griffin. 2007. *Tracking Trash: Flotsam, Jetsam, and the Science of Ocean Motion*. Boston: Houghton Mifflin.

Bryson, Bill. 2004. *A Short History of Nearly Everything*. New York: Broadway Books.

———. 2009. *A Really Short History of Nearly Everything*. New York: Delacorte Books for Young Readers.

Cerullo, Mary M. 2001. *Sea Soup: Zooplankton*. Gardiner, Maine: Tilbury House.

Chasing Ice. 2013. Motion picture. Directed and produced by Jeff Orlowski. New York: Submarine Deluxe.

Committee on a Conceptual Framework for New K–12 Science Education Standards, Board on Science Education, Division of Behavioral and Social Sciences and Education, National Research Council of the National Academies. 2012. *A Framework for K–12 Science Education: Practices, Crosscutting Concepts, and Core Ideas*. Washington, DC: National Academies Press.

Common Sense Education. 2017. "Common Sense K–12 Digital Citizenship Curriculum." www.commonsense.org/education/digital-citizenship.

Cornell University Library. 2015. "Introduction to Research." www.library.cornell.edu/research/introduction.

Cosmos: A Spacetime Odyssey. 2014. DVD, 4 discs. Directed by Ann Druyan, Bill Pope, Brannon Braga, and Kevin Dart. Los Angeles: Twentieth Century Fox.

DeLuca, William V., Bradley K. Woodworth, Christopher C. Rimmer, Peter P. Marra, Philip D. Taylor, Kent P. McFarland, Stuart A. Mackenzie, and D. Ryan Norris. 2015. "Trans-oceanic Migration by a 12 g Songbird." *Biology Letters* 11 (4): 1045. doi:10.1098/rsbl.2014.1045.

Earle, Sylvia A. 1995. *Sea Change: A Message of the Oceans.* New York: Ballantine Books.

———. 2009. "My Wish: Protect Our Oceans." TED talk (video), February. www.ted.com/talks/sylvia_earle_s_ted_prize_wish_to_protect_our_oceans#t-25293.

Fandel, Jennifer. 2007. *Louis Pasteur and Pasteurization.* Mankato, MN: Capstone.

Fleischman, John. 2002. *Phineas Gage: A Gruesome but True Story About Brain Science.* Boston: Houghton Mifflin.

Gianopoulos, Andrea. 2007. *Isaac Newton and the Laws of Motion.* Mankato, MN: Capstone.

Grant, Will, and Rod Lamberts. 2016. "Alan Alda on the Art of Science Communication: 'I Want to Tell You a Story.'" *The Conversation,* March 8. http://theconversation.com/alan-alda-on-the-art-of-science-communication-i-want-to-tell-you-a-story-55769.

Greene, Anne E. 2013. *Writing Science in Plain English.* Chicago: University of Chicago Press.

Haskell, David George. 2012. *The Forest Unseen: A Year's Watch in Nature.* New York: Penguin Books.

Heinrich, Bernd. 2003. *Winter World: The Ingenuity of Animal Survival.* New York: Ecco.

Hoose, Phillip. 2012. *Moonbird: A Year on the Wind with the Great Survivor B95.* New York: Farrar Straus Giroux.

iBioMagazine. 2011. "Shinya Inoue (The Marine Biological Laboratory): Dynamic Mitotic Spindle." YouTube (video), November 19. www.youtube.com/watch?v=gHbL-7JTf4E.

Jahren, Hope. 2016. *Lab Girl.* New York: Alfred A. Knopf.

Johnson, Carolyn. 2015. "Tiny Blackpoll Warblers Make Mind-Boggling Migration." *Boston Globe,* April 1. www.bostonglobe.com/metro/2015/03/31/tiny-blackpoll-warbler-makes-mind-boggling-nonstop-migration/xrfuOBZn7uo5NadrZiV1UN/story.html.

Kamkwamba, William, and Bryan Mealer. 2012. *The Boy Who Harnessed the Wind.* New York: Dial Books for Young Readers.

Kean, Sam. 2010. *The Disappearing Spoon: And Other True Tales of Madness, Love, and the History of the World from the Periodic Table of the Elements.* New York: Little, Brown.

———. 2012. *The Violinist's Thumb: And Other Lost Tales of Love, War, and Genius, as Written by Our Genetic Code*. New York: Back Bay Books.

Keeley, Paige, Francis Eberle, and Lynn Farrin. 2005. *Uncovering Student Ideas in Science: 25 Formative Assessment Probes*. Arlington, VA: National Science Teachers Association.

Kurlansky, Mark. 2014. *World Without Fish*. New York: Workman.

Llewellyn, Douglas J. 2012. *Teaching High School Science Through Inquiry and Argumentation*. Thousand Oaks, CA: Corwin.

Lyson, Tyler R., Bruce S. Rubidge, Torsten M. Scheyer, Kevin de Queiroz, Emma R. Schachner, Roger M. Smith, Jennifer Botha-Brink, and G. S. Bever. 2016. "Fossorial Origin of the Turtle Shell." *Current Biology* 26 (14): 1–8.

McNeill, Katherine L., and Joseph S. Krajcik. 2012. *Supporting Grade 6–8 Students in Constructing Explanations in Science*. Boston: Pearson.

McTighe, Jay, and Grant Wiggins. 2013. *Essential Questions: Opening Doors to Student Understanding*. Alexandria, VA: Association for Supervision and Curriculum Development.

Meriam Library. 2010. "Evaluating Information—Applying the CRAAP Test." Chico: California State University. www.csuchico.edu/lins/handouts/eval_websites.pdf.

Miller, Connie Colwell. 2007. *Marie Curie and Radioactivity*. Mankato, MN: Capstone.

Montgomery, Sy. 2015. *The Soul of an Octopus: A Surprising Exploration into the Wonder of Consciousness*. New York: Atria.

Mowat, Farley. 1963. *Never Cry Wolf*. Boston: Little, Brown.

Munroe, Randall. 2014. *What If? Serious Scientific Answers to Absurd Hypothetical Questions*. New York: Houghton Mifflin Harcourt.

National Governors Association (NGA) Center for Best Practices and Council of Chief State School Officers (CCSSO). 2010. *Common Core State Standards for English Language Arts and Literacy in History/Social Studies, Science, and Technical Subjects*. Washington, DC: NGA Center for Best Practices and CCSSO. www.corestandards.org/wp-content/uploads/ELA_Standards1.pdf.

Newkirk, Thomas R. 2014. *Minds Made for Stories: How We Really Read and Write Informational and Persuasive Texts*. Portsmouth, NH: Heinemann.

NGSS Lead States. 2013. *Next Generation Science Standards: For States, By States*. www.nextgenscience.org/get-to-know.

Norton-Meier, Lori, Brian Hand, Lynn Hockenberry, and Kim Wise. 2008. *Questions, Claims, and Evidence*. Portsmouth, NH: Heinemann.

November Learning. 2015. "Educational Resources for Web Literacy." http://novemberlearning.com/educational-resources-for-educators/information-literacy-resources/.

Parks, Deborah A. 2005. *Nature's Machines: The Story of Biomechanist Mimi Koehl*. Washington, DC: Joseph Henry.

Pearson, Gwen. 2014. "Science Writing Checklist." Presented at the Entomological Society of America National Meeting Lunch and Learn Workshop, November 18, Portland, Oregon. https://entomologytoday.files.wordpress.com/2014/11/writingchecklist2014.pdf.

Planet Earth. 2011. DVD, 6 discs. Special edition. Directed by Alastair Fothergill. New York: BBC Home Entertainment.

Rezendes, Paul. 1999. *Tracking and the Art of Seeing: How to Read Animal Tracks and Sign*. 2nd edition. New York: Quill.

Robberson, Sara. 2012. "The Cell's Mystery." *PRX* (podcast), May 20. https://beta.prx.org/stories/79743.

Rothstein, Dan, and Luz Santana. 2011. *Make Just One Change: Teach Students to Ask Their Own Questions*. Cambridge, MA: Harvard Education Press.

Sheldon, David. 2009. *Into the Deep: The Life of Explorer and Naturalist William Beebe*. Watertown, MA: Charlesbridge.

Shubin, Neil. 2009. *Your Inner Fish: A Journey into the 3.5-Billion-Year History of the Human Body*. New York: Vintage Books.

Sobel, Dava. 1995. *Longitude: The True Story of a Lone Genius Who Solved the Greatest Scientific Problem of His Time*. New York: Walker.

Turner, Pamela S. 2008. *Life on Earth—and Beyond: An Astrobiologist's Quest*. Watertown, MA: Charlesbridge.

Tyson, Neil deGrasse. 2007. *Death by Black Hole: And Other Cosmic Quandaries*. New York: W. W. Norton.

Welvaert, Scott. 2007. *Thomas Edison and the Lightbulb*. Mankato, MN: Capstone.

Wiggins, Grant, and Jay McTighe. 2005. *Understanding by Design*. 2nd expanded edition. Alexandria, VA: Association for Supervision and Curriculum Development.

Wilson, Edward O. 2013. *Letters to a Young Scientist*. New York: Liveright.

Winchester, Simon. 2001. *The Map That Changed the World: William Smith and the Birth of Modern Geology*. New York: HarperCollins.

Worth, Karen, Jeff Winokur, Sally Crissman, and Martha Heller-Winokur. 2009. *The Essentials of Science and Literacy: A Guide for Teachers*. Portsmouth, NH: Heinemann.

Yong, Ed. 2011. "Fire Ants Assemble into Living Waterproof Rafts." *Not Exactly Rocket Science* (blog). *Discover*, April 25. http://blogs.discovermagazine.com/notrocketscience/2011/04/25/fire-ants-assemble-into-living-waterproof-rafts/#.V4jsUFfsdUQ.